Jo
Like A Predator

Jim Rocca

To Kerrie Sullivan
Go for it — Big Time
All The Best

Jim

Copyright © 2013 James R. Rocca

ISBN: 1482317362
ISBN 13: 9781482317367

Library of Congress Control Number: 2013902044
CreateSpace Independent Publishing Platform,
North Charleston, SC

Dedication

To the Silent Mover within all of us
that patiently waits for
the opportunity to become more

CONTENTS

ACKNOWLEDGMENTS

The folks that have done the heavy lifting are Douglas Gorney, our editor, and Trish Rocca, my wife.

Doug did more than edit, he asked the kinds of questions that caused me to continue to make deeper connections and deliver a more comprehensive work. We didn't always agree but the end result is a more complete work with the reader being the beneficiary. My hardworking wife Trish tirelessly labored over the "finished" work to find little points that could be improved. She acted as my sounding board for ideas and generated solid new concepts as well. The beginning of the Introduction is but one such contribution. Trish topped it all by using her graphic arts skills to design the book cover, structured the interior layout and created the illustrations.

Diane Worden, our indexer, who went above and beyond her task by contributing her high-level librarian skills to help us clean up punctuation, grammar and proper word usage. Randy Liefer, our longtime friend and honorary family member (Uncle Randy) provided valuable info and direction in the area of research and operations. My son Justin Rocca was a good source of marketing development and our philosophical tie-breaker not to mention comic relief. Christen Rocca, my illustrious daughter who provides her own brand of practical inspiration. Janel Orgovanyi was the lightening fast technical engineer (magician) who helped us with the tricky tech stuff. Jon Clifford, my son's friend, was our resident internet, social and professional network contributor. Charlie Robert, longtime friend and ace headhunter who helped me get into the recruiting game... special thanks. Bob Russell, longtime recruiter and search firm principal who patiently fielded my questions and quietly works to help out of work people. Roger L. Plunk, good friend and classmate and fixer of the first sentence to the book. Joe Verstrepen, my very close friend and confidant—always there if I need him. Charly Egner, my former business partner in the wind farm industry and good friend. Russell Agee, good friend, former high grade Silicon Valley recruiter and steadying influence. I feel absolutely blessed to know all these phenomenal people and I thank them for all they added to this book but especially to my life.

INTRODUCTION

Like any successful hunter, a job seeker has to have a certain mindset: the mindset of a predator.

He wakes up with a feeling of hunger, a deeper hunger that isn't satisfied with food. He sees the environment with sharp eyes, gauging the climate, selecting specific targets. He assesses the market players, their habits, partnerships, strengths...and of course weaknesses. He sees what he wants and moves purposefully yet cautiously closer. Then he waits for the proper moment. At some point environment, climate, culture, market, strength and weakness come together in just the right combination. He can't tell you when that is because it's more instinct than calculation, but when the moment does come he's ready. He strikes, knowing the outcome is inevitable. There is no doubt the catch is his.

This is the consummate hunter. This is The Predator.

Anyone in today's highly competitive job market needs to develop this kind of confidence, knowledge, capability and motivation. I will take you, step-by-step, to that level. You will become familiar with the habits of the predator, and eventually own that skill set.

Now, let's break down the story above to capture the essence of the master hunter.

What Makes the Predator

1. Knowledge of the environment: the ability to assess strength and weakness immediately—and adapt.

2. Confidence: acquired through countless previous experiences, to navigate through any scenario.

3. Competitive instincts: sensing opportune moments to draw in the prey or strike for maximum effect, depending on your assessment of the current climate.

4. Not being satisfied with anything less than the win.

This is the template for the ideal predator-job hunter that we will explore. Even if you only master some of this knowledge, you will be a better version of who you are now.

Believe it or not, you already possess all these traits. What we are going to do is sharpen them, and use them professionally.

What I want to do is to "teach a man to fish" so that he can feed himself. I expect to develop specific critical thinking skills so that you can plan strategically and carry out effective tactical maneuvers, culminating in a personal psychological transformation that will empower you. These are the essential components of the intelligence of the Predator.

Interviewing an executive is different than interviewing a candidate for a junior-level position. Executives vary in their style. Some start with an aggressive approach, putting the interviewer back on his heels. Some sit back and let the interview come to them. Others vary their approach, tempo and delivery, keeping the interviewer guessing as to what they are up to. But at the end of the day you can bank on one thing —they are all alpha-level predators.

I found the interview process both intriguing and educational. Many times I'd ask to sit in interviews with skilled executive candidates I'd spoken to, even after my job was done. I found it fascinating (and very useful) to witness their expert manipulation of the hiring process. The take-away for me was that if the average person could sit in and see what I saw, implementing even the temperament of these interview masters, his or her chances of getting the job would increase exponentially. In the interview chapter—what I call the brains of the book—I use all the best interview practices I observed in all my years of recruiting to create an interview dynamic that will put you in control of the process.

How I Came to Write This Book

With the economy in a deep hole, I was reading daily news reports about high jobless rates and the difficulty of getting the few jobs that were being offered. What did I know about all this? I thought. Was there anything I could do to help? I had spent many years as both an outside recruiter/headhunter and a corporate, in-house recruiter. I had seen superlative interview techniques first hand, as well as job-hunting approaches, internal back-channel 'research' and tens of thousands of resumés and cover letters. I had recruited for every department in a company, conducted negotiations on every level of offer letters and watched the internal rise of top employees. I realized that "yes," I had a lot to offer the job hunter.

After thinking it over for a while, I compiled all of these insider tricks and tips and created an outline for a book. The topics came easily…but it wasn't enough. The job hunter, I realized, needed more than information. If I was to arm the job hunter, I needed to teach him broader, underlying skills. I needed to help him recognize the subtle, underlying principles of success in the job hunt. The thought that first came to mind was "attitude." If the hunter had the right attitude, I felt, an attitude of aggressiveness that would do it. But no, I soon saw that wasn't enough. The job hunter needed a yet more fundamental tool. What was that? What tool can overcome obstacles? Awareness, that's it. Through awareness, listening, seeing, and sensing we can unlock hidden information. Once those secrets are unearthed they can be used in a question and answer session just like the big boys.

The hunter needs the sharp awareness to ask anyone he encounters in the hiring process the kind of questions that will uncover the information allowing him to address his skill set to the employer's specific needs. On the flip side, the hunter needs to be able to answer the tough interview questions. Comprehensive preparation is the key here, of course, but awareness—internal awareness this time—is again the tool of effectiveness.

I saw that three areas of focus would help deliver the hunter to the goal—the job. First, information about the entire hiring process. They needed the hunting secrets I had in my recruiter arsenal. Second, the right attitude—the attitude that came with the confidence of knowing their skills, their prospective employer and their industry. Third, awareness, a subjective attribute that could not only be developed, in a general sense, but molded to suit the hiring process.

I quickly realized I wasn't just building a job hunting machine. These were also the components for empowerment. The reader of this book will in essence be taking a practical and powerful step toward becoming an enhanced person, a person of power, power over one's life.

The steps involved in this seemingly ground-level-guide to job hunting ultimately connect that concrete, down to earth achievement to an abstract psychological attribute of empowerment.

But there's more.

The three components of information/knowledge, attitude/intention and awareness are capable of yielding a higher level of empowerment (enlightenment). There is no reason why we shouldn't go for that, all out—because in the end it will make our job hunt, our career and our life dynamically successful.

I've written this book for the job hunter, but with the subtle skills of the predator that can catch more than a job. Consciousness—the predator's ultimate weapon—can be unfolded and expanded as a real, everyday experience. It's not like we are developing consciousness as much as we are discovering it. Once we've found it, let's use it—in the interview room, on the job and in every phase of life.

Give it a shot.

How to Use This Book

I wanted to take a moment to explain what's in the book and how best to use it.

There are many different kinds of job hunters. What type you are largely depends on skills you own. Someone with an engineering degree needs to job hunt differently than someone with a high school diploma. As such, I have addressed different job skills sectors:

1. Little to no skilled labor

2. College graduates without specific skills

3. Mature candidates with general skills

4. Skilled and advanced skilled labor

5. Executives

In Chapter 2 – Prepare The Hunter – we break these sectors down and show how best to approach the hunt. Skill development, organization and presentation are the primary steps in preparing the job hunter. Before we work toward skill development, however, we will have to assess our skills honestly from the perspective of the job market by asking ourselves, "What are my marketable skills?" "How much are they worth?" If your honest skills assessment yields a market value in the neighborhood of "minimum wage," then rudimentary skill development is a must.

We address that and list about 50 career choices to give you a broad range of future directions. These are careers that take between 4 months and 2 years to develop. They have a compensation scale of 3 to 4 times that of minimum wage.

Obviously, I have just provided a cursory sampling of what an analysis and a solution looks like for "little to no skilled labor" category. Chapter 2 will construct this type of breakdown for all 5 "job skills sectors". It's rich with realistic options for each sector.

Chapter 3 – Hard & Soft Skills, Resumés & Cover Letters – addresses skill, organization and presentation. Once you are past these chapters you are ready to examine your options in the job hunting process.

Chapter 4 – Internet Job Hunting – will introduce you to channels of social and professional networks, internet job boards and advanced search functions that will help you burrow into the hidden job market. You will also learn how to make friends inside your target companies through social and professional internet tools. It also shows you how to use leading-edge digital technology like SEO principles to brand yourself.

Chapter 5 – Pro-Active Job Hunt – is where aggressive job hunting begins. I like to call this the heart of the book: the "Predator" is born here. Up to now we have been preparing ourselves both objectively through skill development, organization and presentation, and subjectively via goal setting, attitude and awareness. Now, however, we are seeking face-to-face contact. We will strategize our market, industry and sub-industry, select our target companies and locate our new boss. The secrets of the headhunter are revealed.

Chapter 6 – The Interview – we use a refined executive interview model, modified for your skill level that will leave the hiring manager wanting more. Chapter 6 is the brains of the book, and is packed with knowledge and innovation. For the very best results I recommend you re-read this chapter until you really own the 'knock-your-socks-off' interview.

Chapters 8 and 9 – The Offer and Your Counter Offer – we cover every major component of the job offer, including job title, compensation, signing and performance bonus data, stock options and health benefits. We will also cover negotiation of a better offer.

Chapter 10 – Career Track Management – the book takes on an expanded mission. We begin to grow the persona of the future. We differentiate between individual contributors and managers, consultants and employees, and teach effective resumé building techniques. The chapter concludes with techniques for evangelizing your industry for insured future success. This final concept creates linkage with individual branding introduced in Chapter 4.

Chapter 11 – Negotiation Strategy and Tactics – I give the reader the essence of "Counter Point Solutions," a negotiation system I created based on countless negotiations I have conducted. This chapter goes hand-in-hand with Chapter 12 – "Strategic Skills." Both chapters build high-level, hard business skills—the objective cornerstones—for sure and rapid advancement.

Chapter 13 – Awareness – will provide the subjective foundation for growth and advancement. With these objective and subjective precepts in place empowerment is a reality. When we are no longer searching for what is needed to get there but have in fact arrived, we will be living a new life. Step up and take what is yours.

At the End of This Book, Where Will You Be?

You will have combined hard factual headhunter knowledge, secrets and techniques with the subjective components of attitude and awareness, to rebuild yourself as a job hunting predator. Once the job offer is tendered, you will have all the knowledge necessary to maximize the offer through skilled negotiation. After that, you will have both the objective and the subjective tool set to build your reputation, the kind of reputation that makes you a force in your group, company and even your industry. You will be a Class A hunter, a Predator.

In the process of becoming the Predator you will have learned how to use the supreme tool of awareness. While exploring both the outward and inward paths of this powerful tool you will have created something else. You will have become intimately familiar with the foundation of your own self—consciousness. This is not a small thing. Through the masterful use of awareness you will have created the ultimate hunter. It begs the question: What else can you create?

Let's find out.

CHAPTER 1
THE HUNT

During my many years as a Silicon Valley headhunter and in-house corporate recruiter, there was one job candidate that impressed me more than anyone.

The VP-level candidate was being interviewed. He was being interviewed by one of our company's VPs as I sat in. The candidate was positive, friendly, articulate and knowledgeable. He exuded confidence—not arrogant, exactly, but pretty close to the line. It was like he knew something no one else did. In his first question, our VP asked him to summarize his business experience. The candidate softly laughed, smiled and said, "How much time do we have?"

He then became serious and asked, "You've seen my resumé, what specific business experience would you like to know about?"

He stared right at our VP department head, a hint of a smile on his lips. Without speaking another word, he'd just said, "The ball is back in your court. Game on."

Several things happened with this answer:

1. He managed the interview by directing the interviewer to specifics.

2. He didn't stray away from what he'd already carefully included in his resumé—points he had prepared answers for.

3. He is testing the interviewer by silently asking, "You have read my resumé, right?" and "Did you understand what you read in my resumé?"

4. He put the interviewer on notice that he wasn't going be asked questions that were vague or irrelevant.

This subtle psychological control of the session caused the interviewer to qualify his future questions and proceed carefully with the candidate.

It was all cordial enough, but a message was sent right from the start. And in the end, the candidate was at least on an equal footing with the interviewer. On my card, I scored the candidate the winner of the first round.

As the interview progressed the balance of power evened out, but only because the candidate allowed it to. At the end of the day he wanted the job offer, and he knew he had to play nice to get it. Even if later he decided to toss the offer, today he was coming home with his catch.

I've been thinking about that candidate lately. In fact, he helped plant the seed for this book. In my view, today's job hunters lack that kind of confidence, awareness and preparation.

In an interview, a lack of confidence will make the job hunter adopt a submissive role, turning over control of the interview. With a lack of awareness the job hunter fails to recognize key opportunities to market themselves. Interviewers unknowingly provide candidates with information and opportunities they can use to their advantage. Finally, lack of sufficient preparation has sunk many a job hunters' ship. Before entering into any exchange with a prospective employer, the candidate should possess knowledge of their company and respective niche. How much research is enough? I expect I will use about 20% of all the information I collect on a target company, but I never know which 20%.

There's more to getting a job than writing a resumé and showing up at an interview. After all, we don't say "job getter"… we say job hunter. This book is about how to be that hunter.

The reason we go on The Hunt is to come back with something. But it's hard to come back with something if we are timid. Before we begin the hunt—or any part of it—we must have the proper mindset.

In our case, the object of The Hunt is The Job. And even the preparation phase of the Job Hunt must be approached with the unwavering intent of capturing it.

Years of experience have shown me that most applicants are desperate to show how worthy they are of a job. Worthiness issues are common in a job seeker. That can lead them to play a docile role. What they say and do in the interview, their very body language, says, "I need this job. I'll do whatever it takes, even if it's outside of the job description." Right away, we compromise and give away our power…perhaps even some of our dignity. Coming into an interview with a submissive demeanor you are asking to be treated as prey. You can't do that and expect to come home with the catch.

We need to find a way to hold our composure, directing every encounter with our prospective employer so we are on at least equal footing—if not fully in control.

So how can we turn the dynamic around?

It's not enough to grab control by sheer force of will. As I learned in the field of fire, effective control is most often delicate, and balanced.

Control vs. Balance

As a U.S. Army helicopter pilot stationed in Viet Nam, I was on assignment at the border between South Viet Nam and Cambodia during the early stages of the Cambodian Offensive. I had an M.I. (military intelligence) Colonel from Saigon on board one day, accompanied by his intelligence team. We flew into the airstrip closest to the action to get maps, radio frequencies and up-to-date coordinates for the locations of our embattled combat units. Our mission: to visit these units immediately after they had overtaken enemy positions and collect info while it was fresh and useful.

We were on a helipad that was in a line of parked helicopters extending to our right and left, waiting for our team to reassemble so we could go. Suddenly, a chopper exploded eight helicopters down the line, sending a flash of fire, black smoke and pieces of aircraft into the air. Ten seconds later, an identical explosion five helicopters away. The enemy was walking mortar rounds down the line of parked choppers…towards us.

At the controls, my inexperienced co-pilot immediately brought the aircraft to a three-foot hover without warning. Some of our team jumped off the ship. Others jumped on. Everyone thought they were saving themselves.

I was aircraft commander, but I didn't make an attempt to seize the controls. One look at my co-pilot told me he was on the verge of panic. I didn't want to crash the ship.

I keyed my onboard mic and asked, "Are we clear to come back?"

Our door gunners replied, "Clear to come back."

"Coming back," I said, in an even tone.

My co-pilot began hovering backwards, clearing us from the helicopter line.

I keyed my mic again. "Tail clear to come right?"

"Tail clear to come right," said a door gunner.

My co-pilot brought the ship into a parallel position with the runway. He was responding to the indirect orders—and bypassing his emotions.

I contacted the tower for departure instructions. The chatter on our radio was buzzing with a high number of cargo aircraft rarely seen this close to a combat zone and rogue choppers getting out of there without tower clearance. In an emergency, orderliness and calmness are the best ingredients for success, and our tower operator was a complete professional. He rattled off clearance instructions at the speed of an auctioneer.

His instructions came back to us almost immediately, "Helicopter at helipad 3 clear for take-off once C-130 on the runway passes your position." We followed them and departed safely.

It was the balance between experience and fear, in this step-by-step sequence, that allowed us to extract ourselves from deadly harm.

I look back at this experience from time to time for the lesson it offers me. The lesson of respectful control, a control based in balance. This kind of control is gained through the balance of sensitivity and intelligence. In the mortar attack incident, the application of respectful control allowed an inexperienced co-pilot to take responsibility for the saving of lives and convert his panic into the dignity of a "job well done."

Control implies force of will but balance incorporates a blend of heart and mind. By employing a diplomatic focus we can weave our way through someone else's agenda without compromising our own goals. This is the lesson. The lesson of respectful control, an evolution of control, rendering control to be almost invisible except for its subtle influence, converting control from a science to an art. This is the cornerstone of the intelligence of the predator.

Fig. 1.1

From Balance to Empowerment

In a perfect world, your needs are equal to the needs of your prospective employer. Never forget this. You have skills and talents that need to be expressed and developed, and you are looking for the proper environment, the right match. You are interviewing the prospective employer as much as they are interviewing you. You have just as many questions as they do. Your relationship must be on the level of mutual respect if it is to succeed.

Keep in mind, too, that you can ply your skills anywhere. You can't put your talents to use at the cost of your psychology or emotions. In life, the subjective aspects of a situation always outweigh the objective ones.

In the hiring process, you want to proceed with caution. Coming off too strong can scare away your prospective employer. You have to know when to push and when to let your catch run with the bait. It's understandable if you need this job badly to help you put food on the table. You may feel additional pressure because you've been out of work for a long time. But you are more likely to get the job if you come off as self-assured, capable and respectful.

This book isn't about slapping those attributes on like a band-aid for your job hunt and interviews. I want to help you to first realize your value, then to spotlight those values. You already possess all of those confident and positive qualities— and much more—so you are selling yourself short when you approach the hunt with an accommodating mind set. Let's reinvent you, the hunter, not with fake add-ons but with the best of you.

The word I'm looking for is empowerment. In finding and displaying the true job hunter inside you, we will also find the real you.

Three Things to Remember

If you get nothing else from this book I hope you come away with this:

1. The goal is to not be submissive in the Job Hunt, and particularly not in the Job Interview.

2. The tool is Awareness. Outer Awareness provides the questions. Inner Awareness provides the answers.

3. The support system is: Live the dignity of your potential, now.

Let's take a moment to discuss these three items. Number one is self-explanatory. However, item number two has many sides to it. It is a key technique not just in the job hunt but in your entire life.

Fig.1.2

Awareness

Awareness is alertness, or wakefulness. For our purposes here, let's say it's akin to listening. Listen and process what is happening in any interaction during the job hunt and hiring process.

Let's work to activate this aspect of awareness for now. By listening closely to all the people connected to your job hunt and hiring, you will naturally have many questions—take notes. Awareness/Listening is your foundation for inquiry. Excellent inquiry is at the basis of excellent intel (as we used to call it in the Army—tactical intelligence or information). Excellent intel is the cornerstone of excellent decision making. This is why awareness is so important. Once all the information is in, the decision usually makes itself.

We have briefly discussed the importance of outer awareness in providing the questions. Now let's see how inner awareness provides the answers.

Once we have driven your inquiry in the interview to a point that yields solid info, expect a flow of questions to be coming right back at you. These questions may come in short bursts or as a continuous flow. In either case you answer from the same place—awareness. Inner awareness, to be specific. After hearing a question, pause. Check in with your internal self-referral system as a place from which you will answer the question. What you may find is that the question can be answered in a couple of different ways. This naturally causes you to ask a clarification question before you know how you want to answer the primary question, so ask it.

Even if the question is straightforward you will still want to fall back on the self before answering. This technique will allow you to formulate not only the right answer but the right delivery. Be sure to always fall back even if you think of nothing at all. The arrows of your return answers will reach their target better if you draw back your bow. So be sure to let your answers come from that deeper level of awareness.

I was in a job interview and after an hour and a half the interviewer said, "I'd like you to work for us. What is your rate?" Obviously, I had thought of this question before the interview and came up with $50-60 per hour as my answer. But I didn't say that. Instead, just paused for a moment. Then I found myself saying, "We have been discussing this position and my qualifications for over an hour. I think you have a better idea of what I'm worth to you then I do."

The interviewer paused then said, "How's $80 per hour?"

Inside I was jumping for joy. That was over 30% higher than my highest number—but again I paused before answering. I said, "I'm not sure if $80 is too much—or not enough. Why don't we try it for, say, three months, and see where we are then?" That was accepted, and the short-term contract proved to be a smart move. After three months I re-negotiated for more money and a higher weekly hourly limit. And all of it came from answering those key questions from my inner level of awareness.

Psychological Support System

The third item I'd like you to remember is the support system, "Live the dignity of your potential, now." This speaks to our underlying theme of Empowerment. The more you move forward in your professional career, the easier it is to see yourself at a more advanced level. So, when you are talking to anyone on the path of your job hunt or hiring process, carry the dignity of your visualization—the potential "you"—into that exchange. You will naturally show up with more authority and command.

If you have ever read the book or seen the movie, "One Flew Over The Cuckoo's Nest," you will probably remember a scene where several of the mental patients escape for the day and take a boat belonging to one of the doctors at the mental institution. While they are on the boat ready to launch, a dock worker challenges them. They all look ashamed and cannot respond to the dock man. McMurphy, the lead character played so brilliantly by Jack Nicholson in the film, finally turns to the dock man and begins to introduce each and every patient as a doctor. As each patient hears his name with the title of "Doctor," you can see him take on a new air of confidence. Soon, the dock man backs off from his challenge and lets them go.

Life coach Tony Robbins used to teach a system of self-improvement based on "Neuro Linguistic Programming" years ago. In a very basic way this method supported the premise that if you can recall a time in your life when you felt strong, confident and self assured and you mimicked that mind-set and posture you could temporally "channel" that mental state and behavior.

In a similar way, by expressing and displaying the dignity of the potential "you"—that is, the future "you"—you will gain the confidence and empowerment of a better you. You will have created inner strength from yourself by yourself. Now, that's putting your best foot forward. Let this be your support system.

Summary

1. Not being submissive in the job hunt

2. Having intent to capture the job even in the preparation stage

3. Finding a blend between control and balance

4. Using balance to create empowerment

5. Awareness, both outer and inner as the key to success

6. "Live the dignity of your potential, now" as your support system

Elements of confidence, control, balance and awareness serve as pathways to empowerment. And empowerment on both the objective and subject venues lay the groundwork for the persona of the future...

CHAPTER 2
PREPARE THE HUNTER—SKILLS

There is no one size fits all for the job hunter. That is why I have defined five categories or sectors of job hunters. I'd like to illustrate job hunting strategies for each one of them:

1. Little or no skilled labor

2. College graduates without specific skills

3. Mature candidates with general skills

4. Skilled and advanced skilled labor

5. Executives

Let's break down each of these sectors and show how best to approach the hunt in each case.

Little or No Skilled Labor

In a perfect world the more developed your skill set, the more money you will make. Let's start this discussion at a basic level. If you haven't finished high school and you have developed no skills then you most likely will be looking for a minimum wage job.

If this is you, know that county, state and federal resources go into job development programs that are geared for your situation.

After selling one of my businesses I thought I'd try to do something altruistic. I worked at a high school—in the type of government program I just mentioned—with over 2000 kids focusing on high school seniors categorized as "at-risk" to graduate.

I was given about 35-40 students each year who had low attendance, low GPA's (grade point average) and discipline issues. My typical student had a little over a 1.0 GPA, meaning they were averaging about a "D" with all their classes. In the beginning of the year I would send all the other teachers in the school the list of the students I was working with so they would know who to contact if they were having trouble with those students. Many times teachers would come up to me and tell me I was given an impossible task.

With my business background I talked plainly to my students. I asked how they saw themselves in the future. "I don't know," was the answer I usually got. But with a little back and forth I was able to find a career choice for each student. Then we'd write down an outline of that career path. Inside of a few months I had identified 188 career programs within about a 20-mile radius that they could enroll in. And every one of these options had a job placement program.

Certificate Programs

All these career options would train the student to qualify at an entry level position in one of those particular fields. These are positions that generally pay 3-4 times as much as minimum wage. A short program is somewhere between 2-4 months, and nothing is longer than 2 years.

It's an excellent return on investment. If minimum-wage is $7.00 per hour, your gross income for a 40 hour work week in a 50 week year is $14,000. Now, 3 times that is $42,000 per year. And 4 times that is $56,000 per year. Over a 40-year period with no promotions or wage increases (just to keep the math simple on all this) that's minimum-wage earnings of $560,000—compared with $1,680,000 (almost $1.7 million dollars) for 3 times that of minimum wage. If it's 4 times minimum wage, it's $2,240,000 ($2.24 million dollars).

I'd stand on my head for 2 years if I knew it would bring in 4 times my current salary. How about you?

If you are at or near minimum wage now, look at Figure 2.1 for a list of careers I found located at different community colleges around the country. I'll bet you will find more than one career you'd enjoy doing.

Certificate Programs		
Accounting	Webmaster	Culinary Arts
Automotive Technician	Paralegal	Dental Hygiene
Business Communications	Phlebotomy	Medical-Radiology
E-Business	Criminal Justice	Fire Fighter
Network Engineer	X-ray Technician	GIS (Geographic Info Systems)
Network Administrator	CAD (Computer Aided Design)	Heating/Air conditioning Tech.
Help-Desk Specialist	ESL	Jewelry
Restaurant Manager	Electrician	Land Surveying
Graphic Design	Plumber	Meeting & Event Planning
HR Management	Carpenter	Personal Fitness Trainer
Marketing Communications	Surgical Technician	Pharmacy Technician
Sales	Social Worker	Physical Therapist Assistant
Database Administrator	Massage Therapy	Film/Video Production
Office Administrator	Journalism	Management
Psychiatric Technician	Registered Nurse (RN)	Dental Technician
Real Estate Broker	Professional Photography	Vocational Nurse

Fig.2.1

If you tell me, "They don't have that career at the community college near me," I'll say, "Find out where they do and move there." That means a max of 2 years living someplace else for at least 1 million dollars more during your working life. How does that not make sense?

You can do your own research on this at www.salary.com. Key in one of these careers and your zip code and see what comes up. This site will tell you what someone with your specific skill set in your particular region currently earns. If you are thinking of moving somewhere else, key in that city and see what it says.

Cathy was a senior in high school. She had a young child and was on government assistance. At school she had completed a year and a half of credits. Meaning it would take another two and a half years for her to graduate high school. She was one of my at-risk students that year. She was actually very bright and upbeat but I knew there would come a time when she would clearly realize she was not going to graduate high school with her friends—and would drop out of school. So when I was notified by the school that she had dropped out after Christmas break, I wasn't surprised. I immediately called her and asked if she would come to school and give me an hour of her time. She agreed.

We started the meeting with some light conversation then I asked, "What would you like to be when you grow up?"

We both laughed. Then after a long reflective pause Cathy said, "A lawyer."

She said it softly like she'd only shared that thought with a few people, as if she was afraid that people would make fun or her. I have to admit I was shocked to hear her answer. Here sat a high school dropout who needed more than two years to graduate high school, someone who was living on government assistance and raising a young child, saying she wants to be a lawyer. Which meant she would have to complete not only high school but college, too—and then three years of law school. Was she kidding me? But one look at her face told me this wasn't a joke.

I hid my surprise and said, "Well (long pause), lawyers have good communication skills, I know you can speak well…but let's see how well you write."

I pulled up her school records and reviewed the results of her writing proficiency tests. They were excellent. I followed by saying, "There are three schools in the area that have a Paralegal program. I want you to visit each one and tell me what you find." She promised me she would.

I already knew those schools and knew what she would find out. It was actually a test to measure her level of commitment. She passed. Two days later she came back in with the results of her research.

I feel if a person is attracted to a particular career then let's work to give them basic skills to at least get an entry level job in that field. My sense is, if they work in and around their own career choice, they'll find a way to advance. They'll eventually get the break they need. And they'll hear success stories of co-workers who started at their level and rose to a higher position.

Cathy explained to me that the only school she was interested in was the one that offered certification as a litigation assistant. It was just short of two years long but it cost $11,000. We talked in detail then I sent her back to that school and told her to speak to their financial aid people. I told her to mention she was a high school drop-out, raising a young child and living on government assistance. She returned the next day with a big smile on her face saying the financial aid folks found $9,000 worth of grant money for her. They told her she could take out a student loan for the other $2,000 which she could re-pay in small monthly installments after she had a job.

She said she would need a high school diploma or its equivalent to enroll in the program. I gave her the contact info for the local GED office. In less than a week she took and passed the GED test and was accepted into her new school.

Cathy continued with the program and maintained a 3.8 GPA. This was the same young person that couldn't maintain a 2.0 GPA in high school. High school didn't seem relevant to Cathy. This did—and her grades reflected that.

After about a year in the program I got a call from Cathy. She was crying. She said she was not able to understand the details of a particular class and was afraid she was going to have to quit. I calmly explained that the school wants to collect its $11,000 course fee from her, so it had an interest in helping her. I told her the school would provide all the tutoring help she needed to complete the program. I also told her: look into your baby's eyes. Make her a promise that she would never have to rely on anyone else to provide for her.

Cathy promised she would. About six months later Cathy called again telling me she was graduating—and that one of her professors got her a job with an upscale law firm in Palo Alto, California, with a starting salary of $55,000 a year. Now that's what I'm talking about!

My job was done. In all I didn't do much. I just pointed Cathy in the right direction—she did all the heavy lifting. She became The Predator. Each of us has that level of power within us. All the programs are there, ready for us to take advantage of them. We just need to step up and take what's ours.

Certificate Programs – Fine Points

So, a few things happen in these certificate programs:

1. Certificate of proficiency

2. Come away with a career

3. Plug into an entry level job in the career you were seeking

4. You get to be shaped by your field of interest

5. Are automatically enrolled in the schools placement service

6. You get paid well

Some fine points here: Always ask the school what their placement percentage rate is for the certificate program you are enrolling in. A 75% placement rate isn't bad, but with anything less than that you should ask questions.

Sources for Certificate Programs

Fig.2.2

I don't think you should necessarily find programs with the highest placement rate and then enroll in those programs just because they get a lot of people into jobs. At the end of the day you still need to satisfy your own nature. So, go after what you feel is right for you: it should be your passion. If you can't find a career that is an exact match then get as close as you can to it. As time goes by your situation will become fine-tuned until it's a great fit.

Other options for you, if the placement rate sounds low for your particular career choice, are:

1. Perhaps the school doesn't really specialize in your career selection

2. The placement agents are interested in other careers

3. The school never really established strong relationships with the companies that employ people in your career selection

Solutions:

1. Search out schools that offer your career selection nation-wide

2. Research the placement rate at other schools in the area

3. Talk to the companies that hire people in your career and ask them where they get their entry level candidates

This is actually basic information that job hunters can use even if they already have more education or job skills—or need to retrain to get started in a new career.

College Graduates with No Specific Skills

College is a great place to learn general knowledge and critical thinking skills—as well as refine social skills. With a lot of interesting courses to choose from—and so many parties to attend—there isn't much time or emphasis placed on researching solid career choices. Four years later we graduate college with liberal arts or basic science or technical degrees that really require more education before you can launch a professional career. Going into the workplace for what it supposed to be a brief period before getting an advanced degree, people seldom come back. So there you are with a bachelor's degree in psychology, English, business, fine arts, marine biology or sustainable living, looking for a job. In today's economic climate that puts you a small step above people without a degree or skilled work experience—and that advantage is eroded by your student loan payments.

Your best hope is to find a company willing to train you in the insurance business, banking, marketing, loans, sales, business development, etc. You can attempt to start your own business, or enroll in a professional certification program for technical or business skills such as accountancy, computer technology or healthcare. I highly recommend the certificate program for all the reasons mentioned above.

If you are currently in college I suggest you spend a significant amount of time researching career options. Find a career you like or are good at and research the job prospects and overall future of that career. Find out how to qualify yourself within that career so you come into the industry with a marketable job title—even if you have to switch to a certificate program within your own field and take out another student loan. Get a solid enough understanding of that career until you can convince the biggest skeptics—your parents, for instance —that it's a good direction for you to take.

Resumé Building

For those of you who have a clear idea about your career direction, you should know how to "resumé build." It starts with a technical degree, then doing 1 to 3 years of technical work in your chosen field. From there you should return to school for either a higher technical degree or an MBA. The MBA is for the person that wants to shift over to the business side of the industry. With your technical education, work experience and MBA you're positioning yourself for serious advancement. The resumé building component comes from changing jobs about every 3-5 years, taking on new positions that either provide more in-depth career development or broaden your knowledge base. Be sure to read the chapter on "Strategic Skills."

Mature Candidates with General Skills

Here you are. Somewhere past 40 years old, a good provider who's worked hard, raised a family, had savings, a family health plan and retirement fund, a homeowner, possibly and because of the down market you are now out of work, and in the general labor pool. Reviewing your skills, you realize they are general skills in sales, marketing, perhaps management or as a supervisor. You may have even had a technical position. Your resumé looks solid, no gaps in employment, positions of increasing responsibilities and even letters of recommendation. You think I'll find a job right away… yet so far, nothing. Why won't they hire me?

It's an employer's market right now. There are few jobs for candidates who aren't highly qualified. Your general skill set can be replaced by someone with more education—or more up-to-date skills. Someone who is younger, doesn't have a family, will work for less money. From an employer's vantage point that means savings. Savings not only in salary but in health care premiums. Perhaps savings even in training if your replacement had recent training in industry efficiencies.

What can you do?

Your first step is do a candid evaluation of your skill set in today's market. Ask a trusted friend, family member or industry headhunter to help give you a more objective perspective. It's important to have a few data points on something like this.

If your assessment tells you that your skill set is still in demand, read the rest of this book and go for it all out. However, if you discover that your skill set is no longer relevant, or getting there, you must find another way to be of market value in today's economy. That can be a difficult realization, but it's an essential one. If your former work life does not play into your future work life, you must ultimately let it go. You cannot fight a battle on two fronts. The psychological expense is simply too high, so again, let it go. Embrace the future.

Find a way to get excited by new opportunities. You were successful in your previous job — you had drive, tenacity, creativity and a good work ethic. That is not gone, it's just time to redirect it. This is a new challenge. You've faced challenges before—you didn't have a long work career by having more losses than wins. So bring out the champion within you. The game is on the line and you have a team counting on you.

The first thing to do is create a solid plan with a serious chance for success. Toss it around with trusted friends and family, and take notes during the talks. Lots of good info comes out of these sessions. These sessions will inevitably be therapeutic, it's true, but they will also be informative. Treat them as if you are at work: get down to business and get all the info possible out of each meeting. Afterwards, review the info and include the most useful ideas into your plan. When you and your team feel the plan is complete, go for it.

Now let's look at some possible solutions for you situation. The two strongest tools you will have for yourself is consultancy and re-training.

Re-training is primarily covered earlier in this chapter in the section on certificate programs. This is an excellent way to gain up-to-date training, sometimes at little or no cost. Several local and state government-sponsored programs use, subsidize or pay for certificate programs through state colleges, community colleges, technical schools and local employment development agencies as well as other institutions. A search of the web will return many lists of community-based organizations that provide career training at little or no cost.

Community-Based Organizations

Counties—particularly counties in or around large cities—have a number of CBO's (Community-Based Organizations). They all receive state or federal funding for jobs programs. I Googled "job training programs Santa Clara County" and among the items on the first page was a site listing more than 40 CBO's in Santa Clara County, California (the County seat is San Jose) with addresses and phone numbers of each of these organizations. You would be hard pressed to find one of those organizations that isn't either hosting or working in coordination with a local jobs re-training program. A core component of these organizations is offering job training and placement—many of them have long-time ties to local businesses. And for most enrollees, their services are free.

Consultant

Being a consultant in your previous industry is a possibility, but only if you are—or can easily be—an expert in your field, and only if there is a demand for consultants in that industry. If not, move on to re-training. If so, start by researching your competition. Can you provide more value than they can? What makes you or your consulting service unique? Understand that you are thinking of becoming self-employed—what are the cornerstones of this type of operation?

There are three components at the heart of a successful business: substance, marketing and cleverness.

Substance is having comprehensive knowledge and or expertise, and a clear way to convey that knowledge in bite-size pieces that are easily understood by your clients.

Marketing? There are so many resources to find out about marketing yourself, depending on your particular industry that I'm not going to offer suggestion here. You will do well by finding this out on your own.

Cleverness, on the other hand, is the most overlooked, undervalued component of successful business. It begs my attention.

I owned a furniture moving company in the 1970's in Silicon Valley. We did well until we discovered the commercial market—then we did really well. I remember giving a bid to a department head of about 100 employees. At some point in our tour of the different work stations he mentioned, "The most important thing to us is to minimize our down-time. If we lose one day we will have lost several times the cost of this move."

A light went on in my head. I told him right then and there that we would structure the move so it would be done over the weekend in its entirety, and that on Monday morning everyone would be ready for work.

He had a big smile on his face and gave me the job on the spot. I spent the next few days planning how to do it.

The move went like this: the actual relocation of all the workstations and support equipment and furniture items was done on Saturday. I called on quality movers from other moving companies, offered them $2 per hour more than they were getting paid, and bought them lunch, too. I started the move with 40 men, 3 trucks, 100 floor dollies (rented), and several computer carts. Our moving system was well organized: the system moved with the precision of a Swiss clock. We were done before 6pm.

On Sunday our customer brought in their own IT team to connect everyone's computer to the server. Their phone system was completely installed before the move. So, on Monday they were up and running. I sent 4 men over on Monday to go office to office and check to make sure everyone was happy as to how their office furniture and equipment was placed.

I also sent a furniture touch-up guy to smooth over any dings on their furniture. All those men were completely done before lunch. My bill exceeded the estimate by a small margin and not a word was said about it by our client. On top of that they offered to be listed as reference for us.

After everyone was paid I put $5,000 in my pocket, not bad for a weekend in the 1970's. Needless to say, now that I had the formula down, I always led with the statement, "Oh, by the way—we can do your entire move so you won't have any down-time."

Out of 50 moving companies in Silicon Valley we became one of the top 3 commercial movers almost over-night. Life was good.

This story is a perfect example of how a "clever" approach can launch your business with all other components being equal. Question your clients, in-depth, from every angle. Take notes, toss the info around with others and find practical solutions where you can. You will then be in a position to offer a service that has real value. And if you can provide that to your clients—real value—you will be well on your way to operating a successful business.

The beauty of being a consultant is that you work on specific projects that you can either accept or decline. You get paid a fee so your client isn't tied with additional expenses like health or retirement plans. You can work on multiple projects for different companies simultaneously thereby increasing potential income. You can select who you work with on a project to project basis, opening the possibility of extraordinary collaborations that produce leading edge solutions.

If you are in one industry many of your solutions will have a common basis; you can customize a similar solution for another client, having already worked through these challenges in a basic way for someone else.

If you have left on good terms with your previous employer—and by the way, do everything in your power to accomplish that—you can call your company contacts and ask them if they will be a reference for you in your new venture. If they say yes, let them know you'd be happy to work as a consultant for them on a project basis. If they really laid you off due to the economy then there isn't any reason why they wouldn't welcome your experience on a pay-as-you-go basis.

Remember when I mentioned, "Question your clients, in-depth, from every angle…and find practical solutions"? Well, guess what: you already know your previous employer's challenges but now that you have time, research a comprehensive solution and offer to design it for them as a consultant. If they say no even though the solution is sound, you can pitch it to competitor companies, wasting as little time as possible for solving what was probably a common industry problem. This is how you re-invent yourself.

Curving back on my own nature, I create again and again. ~
Bhagavad-Gita

Skilled and Advanced Skilled Labor

Of course, you can also work as a consultant if you are a skilled job hunter. You can do this in one of two ways: you can refer to the sub-topic "Consultant" described earlier in this chapter, or you can contract under a technical consulting firm and be available for dispatch to technological firms that need your skill set. Obviously, you lose a lot of control in option number two; however, you get a chance to meet other technical professionals in your field and see how these different companies work from the inside. If finding a job has been difficult this could be a nice place to ride out the storm.

As a skilled job hunter you have a big advantage. You are probably reading this book because you are out of a job and competition for your skill set is high, or because you want to pursue the development of your career somewhere else. My first reaction is to advise you to connect with a headhunter. Although the technical recruiting business really works from the client's side it's important that headhunters have you in their database and realize you are currently available. Having said that, understand that this method is unlikely to result in a job interview unless your skill set is in high demand. You should be prepared to hunt out your own job.

Chapters 4 and 5 will show you the way to attack that problem. They're written for you.

In Chapter 4, I take you step by step through the act of using online social and professional networks to contact people inside your target companies and befriend them. This insider info will help you get to know key people, general company policies, employee benefits, the hiring process, interviewing methods, company culture and more—all of it absolutely invaluable information in your job hunt.

In Chapter 5—"The Pro-Active Job Hunt"—I show how to best use all this information, gathering it into a spreadsheet and systematically evaluating companies to help you set your best targets.

In this chapter you will learn how to use headhunter's techniques and secrets to locate and contact your prospective new boss. And I'll show you how to use your power to reel him into helping you reach your job hunting goals.

Executives

In a down economic market reporting hierarchies can become flattened. Fewer executives are needed, and it goes without saying that more executives are out of work. Executives not only get paid more than the company average but usually have a larger benefits package and are typically older than the company average, meaning health benefits premiums are higher. It's no wonder executives are cost reduction targets in a recessionary climate.

Before the executive job hunter can re-enter the market he or she will need to find a way to increase his/her perceived market value. How can we do that?

What most executives have going for them is a comprehensive understanding of the industry, an excellent contact base, and an understanding of industry crossovers, including support and collaborative players. All of this opens the opportunity of creating new efficiencies, technological enhancements and complex partnerships, to name just a few possibilities.

Another way to increase your profile and perceived value is to evangelize the industry through blogs, podcasts, white papers, news releases, trade journal articles and books. These landmarks of thought leadership help you establish a brand and, hopefully, a unique persona within the industry. Your original ideas, combined with your level of expertise, can help you launch an exciting new image as an industry pundit, respected and quoted by industry leaders. It's a pro-active approach that, done right, will make it easier to target companies for a leadership role.

That is, if you can tear yourself away from the new life you have created.

Summary

1. We listed the five categories of job hunters, depending on their skill level

2. We detailed the value of certificate programs as a primary option for job hunters with little or no job skills

3. We discussed options for job hunters with college degrees but without specific skills

4. Mature job candidates with general skills were given two strong options—consultancy and re-training. CBO's were discussed as a place to receive free training

5. Skilled job hunters were shown how working for a technical consultant could be a good move for them. The info in Chapter 4 and 5, on internet job-hunting and pro-active job hunting was mentioned as essential reading to re-enter the market

6. Executives found out how experience and knowledge of their respective industry can easily be leveraged making them a talked about authority—thus increasing their name and value in that industry

From a skills perspective this chapter affords solid options for five different types of job hunters. This information, combined with web research and pro-active job hunting techniques and secrets, will serve as a lethal combination in growing the Predator. Happy hunting.

CHAPTER 3
HARD & SOFT SKILLS
RESUMÉS & COVER LETTERS

Skills are a major topic in the job hunt. Let's look at yours.

Now as we mentioned in Chapter 1, this book isn't designed to slap on attributes or add-ons that aren't really in your character. Instead, we want to spotlight the value you already have. In this chapter we'll look at how skills organization can help you do that.

Skills can be generally categorized as either hard or soft.

Hard Skills

Hard skills are skills that can be measured or objectively verified, such as: technical qualifications, accomplishments, education, project completions, quotas met, awards received, deliverables, certifications, years of experience in specific functions, etc.

The place for clearly outlining your hard skills is in your resumé.

Example:

- Senior software engineer with 3 years experience in Oracle database systems
- Financial analyst for 6 years in the semiconductor industry
- Surpassed my sales quotas by more than 20% for the last 4 years

Your hard skills may be in sentence format, phrases or bullets, but any way you list them, they need to be short and to the point. They are a factual item and need little or no explanation.

Soft Skills

Soft skills are subjective in nature, and could include: character, passion, communication, listening, team awareness, problem solving, leadership, initiative, work ethic, etc.

Soft skills are presented best in your cover letter. First they should be simply stated, but then you should provide a short narrative.

Example:

I have strong leadership and problem solving skills. At my last job a group of us were trying to establish a new protocol for accounts receivables. Initially we sat there looking at each other for direction, then I got up and went to the white board and started to ask the group what we didn't like about the current protocols. As everyone spoke up I wrote down a list of their comments. It quickly evolved into a brainstorm session, and as a group we came up with some great solutions.

In this short paragraph your leadership, initiative, problem-solving and team awareness skills have been displayed in context, while your communication skills, passion, character and work ethic have been implied indirectly, yet unmistakably. This paragraph may have generated a question or two for your interviewer as well, providing you with an opportunity to elaborate in the interview and further bring home your value.

Practice writing these short, sample paragraphs. Keep them on hand as option paragraphs for a tailor-made cover letter that highlights skills appropriate for the job you are pursuing. You will insert different stories for your cover letter, of course, depending on the job you are hunting. Never think that one cover letter fits all.

Remember that the purpose of the resumé and cover letter is to get you an interview. If you do them in the right way, the two can deliver a powerful one-two punch.

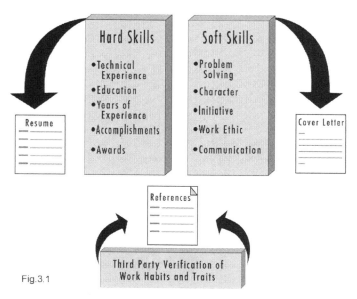

Fig.3.1

Resumé Structure and Purpose

The resumé and cover letter should be thought of as detailed advertisements, presenting your skills with the object of getting you that interview.

I'm not going to tell you how to write a resumé—there are plenty of resumé writing books and services out there that do a great job. Having read thousands of resumés, however, I can tell you about some fundamental do's and don'ts:

1. Be sure to clearly state your **objective**.

    [Example] **Objective**:

    - Product Marketing Manager in the Games Market
    - Sr. Hardware Architect specializing in I C Development for the PC Market
    - Executive Sales Representative in the CRM Industry

You don't want to leave the reader of your resumé wondering what position you are applying for—that's too much work. Your resumé will end up in the trash. Clearly spell out what you are looking for. In a resumé, sharp focus is essential.

The target company is looking to fill a very specific position with a specific job title and a specific job description. Your resumé needs to be a reply to their request and the reply needs to be in "like kind." In large companies the first tier resumé reader is an automated software system. Your resumé is scanned into it, and resumés with the most keyword matches are selected for human review. Keep this in mind when writing your resumé. We will talk a lot more about this in Chapter 4 under SEO.

The resumé reader doesn't want to be a career consultant either, so your resumé should not list more than one position you are qualified for. Do not take a shotgun approach.

We all have more experience and skills than will ever be displayed on our resumé but for now, the resumé reader isn't interested in that additional data. If you have worn many hats in the past and want them to know this, wait until the interview to reveal that. And if you do the resumé right, you will have an opportunity to do that. (Making sure it's <u>relevant</u> information, of course.)

And write a resumé for each of the different skill sets you are experienced in.

I know someone who has five resumés. He clearly knows the value of pinpointing his skills.

2. Make sure your **technical skills** are mentioned right under your objective.
    You have stated in the objective what position you want, now demonstrate what qualifies you for that position. List your technical skills in bullet format. After each technical skill include the amount of experience for that skill in time.

    [Example] **Technical Skills** Summary:

    - Oracle database proficient – 2 years
    - Financial Analysis – 3 years
    - Product Marketing Manager – 4 years

    This helps the reader bracket your skill range.

3. After you have stated your objective and listed your technical summary you are ready for the **work experience** section. Always start with the dates employed—e.g. February 25, 2001 to June 7, 2003—followed by the name of the company, its location (city and state only) and your official job title.

[Example] **Work Experience**:

February 25, 2009 to June 7, 2012 – ABC Inc. – Chicago, IL – Operations Manager

Be accurate with this info: at some point your prospective employer will order a background check. That process is usually outsourced, and the background checking company will adhere strictly to the info on your resumé. Any misinformation in this area can be considered fraud and constitutes grounds for an immediate dismissal. The background check will be discussed in great detail in Chapter 7.

After listing dates, company, location and job title, briefly describe what you did there. This description can be in bullets or sentence form. You will get a lot more on a page if it's a run-on sentence with commas delineating your job duties.

Here are a couple of examples from my own resumé. The first is a listing of my duties at a land acquisition company where I was VP. The second is a software development firm that I did recruiting and negotiations for, first in an up market and then in a down market.

Management of multiple Land Acquisition projects in the Wind Industry. Duties consist of interviewing, hiring, training, deploying, field training, monitoring, assisting new and experienced land agents in difficult cases. Also, direct interface with client representative in consulting and management capacity regarding strategy, budget, personnel, land work process, legal process, deeds, contract writing, documents, progress metrics, detailed reports, mapping, etc.

Recruitment functions for the entire company in every department. Negotiation of reduced compensation packages with every Sr. Executive nation-wide. Negotiation of all Sr. Executive severance packages. Re-negotiation of contracts for the purpose of cost reductions in B2B partnerships, office space leases, outside recruitment agencies, contractor agencies, etc. Maintained and presented employee stock reports for Board of Director approval. Compiled metrics for headcount, RIF, legal demographic, benefits, etc.

Remember, space is at a premium. A resumé should rarely be two pages. The rule of thumb is that hard facts go on the resumé while soft facts are on the cover letter. The cover letter is a good place for you to be eloquent, but it should never exceed one page either.

4. After the work experience section, enter your **education information**. Start by listing your degree(s).

    [Example] **Education**:

    • B.S. in Computer Science
    • B.A. in Accounting
    • M.S. in Computer Science

If you have more than one degree list the highest first. If you have multiple undergraduate or graduate degrees only list what matches your objective—if your master's degree seems like overkill for the position you have applied for, omit it.

I know someone that had three graduate degrees but wanted a medium-level county position so she only listed her undergraduate degree and got the job. She told me her graduate degrees would have forced the county to pay her above the pay scale for the position—she was sure that would have disqualified her.

After listing your degree mention the name of the school and the year you graduated. Be absolutely accurate in the Education section so that there is no discrepancy in the background check. It's worth calling the school to ask them how your degree is titled or described in their records. Use those exact words on your resumé to avoid any misunderstandings.

5. If you have other noteworthy distinctions such as military service awards, major academic honors, civic commendations or business achievements, this is a good place to list those in bullet format. I encourage you to mention these sorts of distinctions. Hiring managers are almost always interested in a candidate's unique or diverse life experience.

As a former U.S. Army helicopter pilot I can't tell you how many interviewers have asked me about that. I wouldn't doubt that I may have edged someone out of an interview on this fact alone.

It comes down to marketing. Use what you have in your resumé and cover letter to differentiate yourself from your competition.

References

An interview is really self-validating. If you display the awareness, control and confidence of the predator, managers will pick that up. That's why a good hiring manager will also be interested in 3rd party verification of your work habits and traits. When it comes time to provide a list of references make sure they are previous supervisors. The hiring manager will not be interested in co-workers at the same level as you.

Never assume your previous supervisors will be good references. Call or better yet meet with them. Tell them about your new job pursuit. Gauge their reaction. Are they genuinely happy for you? Happy enough to speak about you in a positive light? Do they appear surprised by your announcement? If so, why?

Your references have to be rock solid. They need to be 100% on your side. Even a marginal reference can be damaging. It tells your prospective hiring manager that your former supervisor wasn't too impressed with your work. If you have any doubts as to whether they will be a strong enough reference for you, drop them. Find someone else. You cannot take a chance with this.

Cover Letter Structure and Purpose

The Cover Letter is very different than the resumé. It is essentially an essay on why you should be considered for the job. You have already mentioned your hard skills in the resumé; now it's time to discuss your soft skills. Let's take a moment to look at the list of soft skills we mentioned earlier.

There are many different topics here. You can display character traits such as integrity, strong work ethic, passion for the job at hand and initiative. You can discuss your goals and achievements. You can write about functional skills like team awareness, communications skills, problem solving attributes and leadership.

For the best results these traits and skills need to be corroborated by a previous employer. Here is where you invite the reader to see copies of any letters of recommendation or "thank you" letters from previous employers or customers.

If you can't do this then give a real-life example of your skills or traits. Tell a very brief story of how, in the context of your job, you exhibited one or more of your abilities or special characteristics. In this way you add color to the traits you've listed instead of just blandly explaining them.

Example:

At my previous company it was almost 5pm when my team leader called an emergency group meeting. One of our client's systems had malfunctioned, causing the rest of the system to provide faulty data. Out of the six team members present two of us volunteered to stay after hours to work through the problem. At around 3:30am we were able to have the client's system up and running at full capacity. The client never knew all we had to do for this to happen. I was back on the job the next morning at 9:30am—only a little late—to do my part in a team-wide project we were all working on.

Stories are powerful, and one like that can be very powerful in getting you to an interview. Don't forget, the goal of the resumé and cover letter are to get you an interview. If you maintain awareness of these short-term, immediate goals, your big objective—getting the job—will be yours.

Integrity and honesty are high on the list of admirable traits that employers look for. Be sure to discuss them in the cover letter. Include your long-term goals and/or the reason you choose this particular career. Make a clear link between your goals and how working for this company will help you reach them. Show that you understand their goals, based on your research of the target company or niche industry—and unite your goals with their goals.

If there really is a match between you and the company it should not be hard to show an interest in their goals and achievements. You should be able to find many areas of compatibility, and write pages about the things your mission shares with theirs. (If you do write pages, be sure to edit and cut it down to one page.)

Display your company research, your knowledge of the company and its niche industry both from a technical standpoint and their position in the market. Know the company's products and services. Understand where they rank in their niche industry and what the industry thinks of them. Do your homework.

Summary

1. We organized our skills into hard and soft skills

2. Hard skills are listed predominantly in the resumé

3. Soft skills are unfolded eloquently in the cover letter

4. The resumé structure has 5 parts: Objective, Technical Skills Summary, Work Experience, Education and Achievements and for best results should be displayed in this order

5. Check out your own references to insure they are rock solid

6. When it comes to resumés, a sharpshooting (highly focused) approach works much better than a shotgun (broadly based or scattered) approach

7. In the cover letter you want to display your soft skills or traits as a series of mini-stories

8. For maximum effect, corroboration from previous employers or letters from customers are powerful 3rd party tools

9. Never forget that the sole purpose of the resumé and cover letter are to get you to the interview

This chapter is a powerful step toward getting you the job because it tells you what you need to do to get the interview. We've demystified the purpose of the resumé, cover letter, references and letters of recommendation. By understanding how to organize your current skills into two basic components, hard and soft skills, you are in a position to present those skills purposefully and effectively.

You've done your preparation and selected your prey. Now you are ready to start the hunt.

CHAPTER 4
INTERNET JOB HUNTING

Ever gone online to check your email or do a simple search, only to find an hour later that you haven't done either? Then you know how easy it is to get sidetracked while visiting the web. When you are job hunting you are on a mission. The web is an essential tool for that mission. The question you have to ask yourself is, "am I controlling it, or is it controlling me?"

The internet is a tool, use it as such. Step into the web environment with a specific goal and then carry it out. If you want to play afterwards that's fine, but when you are job hunting, you are hunting. So be the predator.

In this chapter we will drill down into how we can best leverage online tools and networks for locating job opportunities, company research, social and professional networking and marketing yourself— attracting employers by creating and posting content that shows us in the best light. Some of what we discuss in this chapter will have multiple application, for example: with your personal profile on LinkedIn you are both developing a professional network tool and marketing yourself.

Company Research

Let's take a look at how we can gather company info. What are we looking for?

Some areas to search that will help you select a target company for your hunt are: company financials, size, locations, industry rankings or titles, and names of key employees. Depending on the specific nature of your search there are several websites that have this kind of data.

These sites are a good starting point: Yahoo Finance (particularly under the "Investing" tab), Hoovers, ZoomInfo, OneSource and Manta. Each of these sites have a particular way of compiling company data. Test drive them so you can match your style to their structure. Note that you will get data that is strong in a particular field and weak in another, so it's not a bad idea to cross-check collected data with other sites. Of course, you will find other sites on your own that have this type of info as well—by all means use them if you find them useful. You will soon establish a routine that fits your research style, making your company research efficient and snappy.

Job Opportunity Research

As far as job listings on the internet go, there are the big job boards like Monster, CareerBuilder, Indeed or Dice (specializing in technical jobs), as well as Craigslist; smaller, more focused or affinity-based job boards like trade sites and college alumni job boards; government (federal, state or county) job sites; and social or professional network sites like LinkedIn, Facebook or Twitter. The web sourcing options are endless.

I've read in some other job hunting books that the job boards are dead—not so! They may not be what they once were because all jobs are not posted but they are still alive and doing well. In job-seeker surveys, between 20% to 40% of respondents say they found their job on a job board. What really matters is not the number of jobs that are posted there but the skill set of the job hunter.

If you are a software developer your chances of finding a job on the big-name job boards is good. As we said in Chapter 2, marketable skills combined with solid networking will keep you employed. And a good attitude doesn't hurt, either.

I'm not going to spend a lot of time discussing how to use job boards. They're self-explanatory—visit any job board and you will understand it immediately. I will however, suggest that you choose job boards that are more specific to your industry and skills, and always upload your resumé.

You should also use Google. Google's advanced search functions let you use different combinations and related searches to hone in on your target job. Take notes of the keywords and phrases you're using, highlighting those that yield the most useful data. Then use those combinations to conduct searches on other search engines as well. Do it daily. You will establish a routine that will become second nature to you. It's not a bad way to start the day.

Social and professional networking, involve a marketing component that makes it deserve special consideration. Let's start by discussing LinkedIn.

LinkedIn

Nestled between the two fundamental online tasks of research and marketing is the king of professional networks, LinkedIn. A unique hybrid of social networking, business application and marketing, LinkedIn deserves to be discussed on its own.

I'm going to point to useful tools within LinkedIn but there simply isn't space within this chapter to uncover all the applications this professional networking tool has available. I highly recommend you get your hands on a copy of *How To Really Use LinkedIn,* by Jan Vermeiren and Bert Verdonck. These guys go into all the bells and whistles hidden in this tool. It's extraordinary.

LinkedIn isn't a laid-back environment like Facebook or Twitter. That hits you right away. It becomes clear immediately that this site's purpose is to conduct business.

The first thing you're directed to do is build a professional profile. Before you start this task, ask yourself, "What do I expect to accomplish with this profile?" Give it some thought.

I'm sure most of you already have a LinkedIn profile. Revisit it and see if what's on there is exactly how you want to be understood, professionally. Think about your profile not so much in terms of "What kind of job do I want?" as much as "What career do I want?"

In building your profile you will actually be installing the first cornerstone to your brand. We will discuss this in great detail shortly but for now know it's important to have a long vision in crafting your profile.

The next step is selecting the members to your network. This should be done carefully. Be selective in who you invite as well as how many contacts you invite. The group of friends you socialize with may not be the ones you would build a business with, so be selective. LinkedIn is a site where you build your career.

The kind of folks you invite should be people that support you career treatise the one you declared in your profile. Consistency is important here. As such, start with a handful of people above your current "pay grade" and a handful of bright up-and-comers at your career level. Let that small core group set the standard you use to invite others.

Communicate with those core invitees to let them know what kind of goals you have for your LinkedIn profile. Ask them if they know others that fit the formula. In this way, you are building a small but quality-rich group that resonates with your career mandate. These are the type of folks who will produce quality contributions to group discussions and can help launch your career.

How do you create a small discussion group that advances your objective?

You will want to start with the kind of people you have invited but you don't want to invite them to a group that is simply a duplicate of your general group. I can't tell you how many groups I've turned down because they have no goal. Have a clear theme and purpose for the group, and when you invite people to your group make sure they know it. The group invite should have a descriptive title, a goal and the first topic for discussion.

Here's where you'll have to do your homework. Chapter 12, Strategic Skills Development, will help you create relevant topics for any industry-related discussion. I outline a four-step process to build your business strategy I.Q.: research, analysis, creation and testing. Your LinkedIn group is where you test your ideas.

If this seems too advanced for now, feel free to toss around industry topics that are currently in the news. Just make sure you have studied at least some aspect of a discussion point so you can deliver an opening statement to kick things off. If you've invited bright, informed, dynamic people into your group, you shouldn't need much kindling to ignite their theories.

With these three items you have created an excellent beginning:

1.   a solid career oriented profile

2.   invitees that are talented and excited about the industry

3.   a small discussion group with a goal and lead off topic.

With this you are equipped for success. For those of you that have been in the industry for a while, restructuring your goals, profile and small discussion group will show you are adaptive to modernization for the sake of advancement of yourself and your industry. That's quite a statement, make it your mantra. Add it to the code of the predator.

Those are some of the LinkedIn basics, but let's touch on a few other tips that will let you get more out of LinkedIn:

When you look at someone's LinkedIn page, check out their "Viewers of this profile also viewed…" This is a good way to expand your group. These profiles are often people in your field with similar career goals.

Click on "Companies" at the top of your home page to search the companies you want to target. Click to "Follow," this will create a shortcut to get back to their profiles. LinkedIn also has a notification system that tells you when jobs are posted at the company, or when someone is hired or departs— all useful info.

On a target company's page you can click on the "Employee Insights" tab to see "New Titles" and "Departures". You can contact departed employees to collect valuable data about hiring managers, interview methods and corporate culture, just to name a few.

Under the "Careers" tab on the company site, you can access a listing of employees. You can connect with and contact them to collect valuable data on company health benefits, common stock option structures, bonuses, you name it.

Contacting current and former employees is how you collect valuable insider data to help you decide what companies you want to target, how you should prepare yourself for interviews and what to expect to be offered. This is such a valuable intelligence resource it cannot be overlooked.

Be sure to experiment with the "advanced search" feature. It's an excellent way to find exactly the kind of contacts you are looking for and it also has a "sort" feature and "save search" button.

For around $20 a month LinkedIn has a "Job Seeker" service. The name says it all.

This should give you an idea of the many ways you can use LinkedIn, but again, for more in-depth knowledge I strongly recommend Vermeiren and Verdonck's book.

Marketing

Here's the two-word bottom line on modern marketing: **Brand yourself!**

Building a brand is the best way to use the internet for your individual career advancement. I discussed some of these principles in the "Executives" section of Chapter 2, but now let's take a closer look at branding yourself from the vantage point of someone breaking into the industry.

I recently spoke to Jon Clifford, a good friend of my son's, about how he got a great job in a company he really wanted to work for. He told me how he used Twitter, Facebook and LinkedIn in combination to strategically position himself for success.

Jon had thought about a career at a leading edge company, hopefully working in internet marketing (a clearly defined goal). He constructed his LinkedIn profile to reflect his long term career objectives. On Twitter, Jon had made mention, when appropriate, about his internet marketing aspirations.

One day he saw a message on Twitter from a friend announcing that her company was seeking to fill a sales and marketing position. The company was a content marketing software firm—just the kind of company Jon was looking for. He immediately tweeted back his interest in the position.

In the next few days Jon watched as several new people began viewing his LinkedIn profile, started to "follow" him on Twitter and friended him on Facebook with one common thread: they were all from the company where his friend worked.

Jon quietly watched as a new network was born. Then he got the call. One of the company's representatives scheduled a Skype call for an interview. Soon afterwards he was flown out from New York to Colorado for an interview. A few days later he was offered the job.

In talking to Jon he felt blessed to get a job right in the middle of his field of interest. I felt it was to his credit for shaping his own future. As he put it to me, "It's all free—you'd be crazy not to take advantage of it."

Jon personifies the intelligence of the predator.

I really love this story because it's a perfect example of how to adeptly align a variety of social and professional networking sites to broadcast one message. This is **branding**.

Your Brand — Your Site

Having your own website is an essential element in building your brand, a virtual office into which you can funnel all your professional contacts to give them a fuller understanding of who you are.

That can seem like a big project, but I've encountered three free services that let you quickly put together a "splash page." All of these sites are easy to set up, and fun, too. They link easily with LinkedIn, Twitter and Facebook and other networks.

About.me has been around since December 2009 and was acquired by AOL almost immediately. The look and feel is beautiful.

BUILDING YOUR BRAND

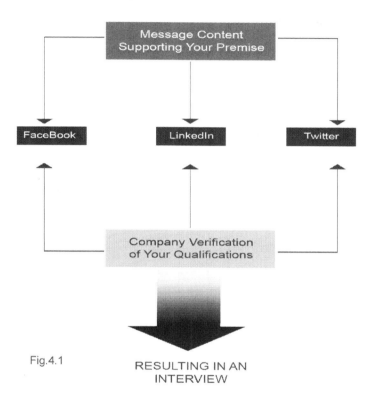

Fig.4.1

Flavors.me was launched in January 2009 and appears to be laid out as nicely as About.me. Information is stylishly done without a sense of clutter.

Vizify.com launched in 2011 with a different look and feel than the other two platforms. Its infographic–style user interface displays your information as a collection of labeled bubbles connected by lines. Click on a bubble and it expands, displaying details about where you have lived, what schools you have attended, where you have worked, etc.

Search Engine Optimization

Now that you have your own site you will need to become fluent in SEO. Search Engine Optimization is the art of building a website with keywords and phrases that give you a better position in searches done for your product or service. Michael H. Fleischner has written an excellent book on the subject entitled, *SEO Made Simple: Strategies for Dominating the World's Largest Search Engine.*

A major corporation's first method for finding qualified job candidates outside of their firm is to launch a web search through search engines using keywords and phrases. Think of it as a contest, where one set of keywords and phrases tries to match up other sets of keywords and phrases. The resumé, CV or personal website with the most matches, wins. For the internet job hunter, wordtacker.com, adwords.google.com or "related searches" on Google are key to expanding your keyword vocabulary so you can attract the right kind of employer.

Once you have a strong list of words and phrases directly or indirectly related to your career you need to know where to put them. The obvious places are in the title and body of your resumé, of course, but hidden in the html code are meta tags (Google or YouTube them to understand how to do this). By installing those keywords there you are "optimizing" the chances of your resumé jumping to the head of the line.

It's easy to prove the value of optimizing your site. Google using keywords that an employer would use to find you, see where you come up in that search. Make the changes, placing the most likely keywords and phrases to find someone with your skill set in the content and the meta tags, then Google it again. Notice a difference? Continue to adjust until you are satisfied.

This a fraction of the information contained in SEO Made Simple by Michael H. Fleischner.

This is how the modern predator uses the digital landscape to his or her advantage.

Summary

1. While on the internet, stay focused—you are there to locate job opportunities, do company research, and market yourself through social and professional networks

2. Some good sites for company research are: Yahoo Financials, Hoovers, ZoomInfo, OneSource, Manta and LinkedIn

3. Top job boards are: Monster, CareerBuilder, Indeed and Dice (tech jobs)

4. Other job boards: trade or industry-specific, alumni and government (federal, state and county) job boards

5. Advanced search functions on Google can sometimes help locate jobs more effectively than hunting on job boards

6. LinkedIn is the king of professional networks, a hybrid of social networking, business application and marketing

7. Before you create your profile on LinkedIn know exactly how you want to be understood, professionally

8. Three fundamental steps for your LinkedIn presence: a solid, career oriented profile, adding connections who are talented and excited about the industry and inviting the right people into a small discussion group with a goal and lead off topic

9. *How To Really Use LinkedIn,* by Jan Vermeiren and Bert Verdonck is an excellent book on the fine points and tactics of LinkedIn

10. Branding yourself is the best way to market yourself on the internet

11. The Jon Clifford story is a perfect example of triangulating Twitter, LinkedIn and Facebook to convey a uniform message of career objectives

12. Build a "splash page" at about.me, vizify or flavors.me to help organize and promote your brand

13. Promote it and make sure the right companies find it by becoming fluent in SEO

14. *SEO Made Simple: Strategies for Dominating the World's Largest Search Engine,* by Michael H. Fleischner is a great book for becoming fluent in SEO technology

15. If employers are using keywords and phrases online to find qualified job candidates then you need to match their keywords and phrases in your resumé, CV and website to be found—it's as simple as that

The internet is a powerful job hunting tool but you must be focused and in control to maximize your effectiveness.

Understand how you want to be known professionally and deliver that message. If you have several talents, closely assess and prioritize them. Try to select one skill set and use the others as support skills. You are always better off if you start by marketing one thing.

You can begin with a few descriptive sentences then boil it down to one sentence, then a short 3-5 word phrase. That's your message. Build your professional profile around that short, declarative statement. You can now use all the tools—LinkedIn, Twitter, Facebook and of course your personal website—to announce and promote your brand.

Don't forget to use SEO principles to help shape and maximize the impact of your message. In the end you will be poised to be a name in your field of interest. Future job hunting will be on your terms. That's the mark of the predator.

CHAPTER 5
THE PRO-ACTIVE JOB HUNT

As powerful as internet job hunting can be, its own nature deems it predominately a passive system. To build the job hunter of the future we need to add a predominantly pro-active system to our arsenal. With this we will have created the complete job hunter.

If this book is about one thing, it's being pro-active. The job you are looking for in the companies you like is not going to be posted on a job board, a newspaper or some career center bulletin. You are the predator: you have to hunt for it.

You will need to find the industry you want, then the niche industry within it, then a group of target companies, then the right department or group—then your new boss. This pro-active progression is the professional way to go about this business of job hunting.

What is being delivered here is really a state-of-the-art job hunting system more successful than any other method out there. We have come to this point by the logic of "economy of effort." Use it and you won't waste time or let your focus be distracted by jobs that "might" work for you.

Now let's get to work.

Focus The Hunt — Selecting A Niche Industry

Your skill set should work especially well in a particular industry. You should already know which one. If not, take time to figure it out.

Within any industry there are micro or niche industries. Drill down into your desired industry and locate those niche industries. Select the one that is as close to perfect for your skill set as possible.

If you have high proficiency in more than one skill set, locate an appropriate niche industry for each of your skill sets. Also, write resumés highlighting each skill set separately: if you have 3 different skill sets, you need 3 different resumés.

Once you have located the appropriate niche industry for your particular skill set, research the companies in the selected niche industry. The Yahoo Finance pages list companies by sector, industry and sub-industry. You can also find them on Hoovers.com, ZoomInfo.com, OneSource.com, Manta.com or any other websites where companies are briefed.

By all means go to the individually selected company's home page to collect data as well. However, note that an independent website like Yahoo Finance, Google, Hoovers or ZoomInfo are less likely to be biased toward the selected company. After studying the niche industry companies, you are ready to select three companies that best fit your skill set.

Selecting Your Target Companies

Several factors come into play in selecting your top three companies. They have to be a good match for your skills, of course, but the culture needs to be compatible, too as well as opportunities for advancement. A good salary increase schedule, benefits, training, stock options, bonuses, etc. need to be right also.

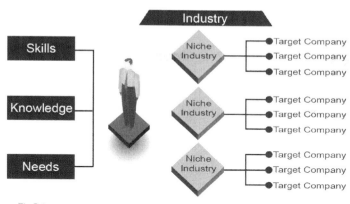

Fig.5.1

If you are looking at an executive position you will also have to consider whether it will let you be part of the e-staff meetings, participate in the decision-making process, give you a distinct area of responsibility and all executive perks, and even whether there is a pre-determined severance package.

Some of these things will be almost impossible to know from the outside but you should have a comprehensive list drafted anyway. Be ready to find out as much as possible when you are talking to someone inside the company. Of course, use LinkedIn, Twitter, Facebook, etc. to find and contact those inside people.

Spreadsheet as much as possible so you can compare your selected companies at a glance and identify what company provides which advantage. Don't forget to include the info collected through your friends in the target companies, using the internet technique we discussed in the previous chapter. It will be rewarding to see all your reconnaissance and espionage compiled in one master location.

After researching your niche industry you should choose three companies that you feel really good about working for.

Now, we can get to work growing our list of prospective employers from three companies to 40.

Why 40 Companies?

You want to end up with a target of forty companies. You are selling them something, after all—yourself—and you want a big enough base group to be successful.

Sales numbers work in accordance with a numbers matrix. If you are selling a product in a logical market—a market that can use your product and pay your price—then you will need to contact between 25 and 50 prospective buyers to make one sale. Sales research shows that contacting, say, 40 buyers will generate five to seven interested buyers, and, out of that, one or two actual buyers. This is why it's important for us to have 40 companies in our target group.

So why did we do all that work to narrow our target down to three companies? What I like to do on Yahoo Finance, Hoovers, ZoomInfo, OneSource, Manta or another corporate information site is choose one of the three companies initially selected and bring up its competitors. Then I research the competitor company and find its competitors. Clearly there will be overlap, but listing all these companies on our spreadsheet, eliminating any duplicates and checking to make sure they are in our niche industry, we will eventually get to 40.

Now it's time to start The Hunt.

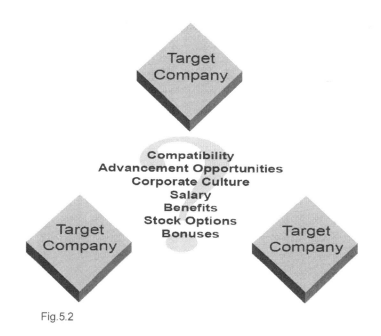

Compatibility
Advancement Opportunities
Corporate Culture
Salary
Benefits
Stock Options
Bonuses

Fig.5.2

Who to Contact — HR vs. The Manager

Human Resources is generally thought to be the central contact point for the job seeker. Not so. HR receives job orders from managers throughout the company. They can't be expected to know the finite details of all the open positions. There is no way for them to know if there is need for your skill set, especially if the job has not been posted or requested by a manager.

You have to contact the one person in the whole company who will be most excited about your skill set: your New Boss.

We're not talking about the department VP, but rather your new direct Manager. This is the one person who can most appreciate your talents and be most motivated to employ your skills. The operative word here is motivated. Others in the hiring process may find your skills interesting or commendable but the hiring manager is in a different position: he is the one who has to produce deliverables. He also knows through years of experience who he needs to do that with. If your skill set resonates with him, if it's a match for his assignments, then he will push to bring you on board. That level of knowledge and motivation trumps HR.

Finding Your New Boss — Insider Secrets - Recruiter's Tactics

How pro-active are you prepared to be? It's time to give you—the job hunter—some insight into what we recruiters do to worm our way through a company. The tactics I'm about to reveal are not for everybody. But I feel I'd be remiss, in a book about aggressive job hunting tactics, if I didn't share these techniques and secrets.

By looking on the company website you should find some of the people heading your department. VP and below is what you want. You can also look at some of the other websites discussed earlier—Hoovers, Yahoo Finance, LinkedIn, ZoomInfo, Google, Manta, OneSource, etc. Start a list of the folks in your department within your target company. When you have two names or more call the company. Tell the receptionist you are an outside contractor who was supposed to contact someone in _____ department about some work.

You then say, "I know it wasn't _____ (use one of the names on your list) and I know it wasn't _____ (the next person on your list). "Who is the person that runs _____?" (Name the specific area that you are looking to work within.)

If it's a small company the receptionist may know that person and give you their name directly. He or she may even offer to transfer your call to them. If so, be sure to ask for that extension number "in case you get disconnected." You should now have the direct line of the department manager.

If it's a large company they may have to forward you to an administrative assistant in that department. If so, repeat what you said to the receptionist. If asked, "Who told you to contact this person?" use one of the names from the same department at a competitor company, i.e. "Bill Johnson at XYZ Inc. did." This will give you immediate creditability, authenticity and urgency.

If you are reluctant to play this game, there are other options. Recruiters will sometimes buy "research." Meaning, they will outsource the task of getting names of specific job titles in particular companies, including title, name and phone number, at $40 to $60 per name. You can contact recruiters and ask them who they use for research in your particular geographic area.

They will ask you why you want that info, so be direct. They may have a job order that matches your skill set.

In addition to buying research they may be using other sources to conduct their research, such as Microquest Directory (mqc.com). This is an expensive candidate database that lists companies by industry and sub-industry, with a significant number of names for each company by department.

You may befriend a recruiter who will let you view the directory. Don't expect that a recruiter will want to represent you, however. Any good recruiter knows the process works from the direction of the client company, not from the candidate's side. The recruiter gets job orders from the client company, than they search out the appropriate candidate. The company pays for this search 30 days after the candidate is hired. So you should be prepared to do your own search for the best results.

As the predator, be aware of the power you hold. Explain to the recruiter that you will be talking to companies that don't have posted job orders, and that in exchange for his help you are willing to forward information about those non-posted job orders to him.

Keep in mind that recruiters specialize in specific job titles, so you may have to talk to a few of them before one of them gets excited about your "deal." I talked to one successful recruiter who told me he occasionally does pro-bono work to help candidates with a hiring manager's contact info—so yes, it happens.

Contacting Your New Boss

Once you track down your prospective new boss, call him or her. Introduce yourself, giving them your title and company you work for or used to work for. If you are a student tell them your major, the school's name and when you are graduating. Then tell them why you're calling.

Start with, "The reason I'm calling you specifically is, I'm looking for a job that will challenge my talents. I'd like to get your feedback as to where I should be looking. Is it possible to have a cup of coffee to talk about this?"

The manager will say yes, no or maybe—all of which translate into Yes. The only real No is when he hangs up on you.

If he says, "I really don't have time or I'm not qualified to direct you," your comeback should be, "I'll be working in this industry doing the same stuff you are doing and I know we will run into each other sooner or later. I'm sure it can't hurt to share contacts from a network prospective we can mutually benefit from. After all, I am currently talking to lots of companies—I can easily keep an ear open about job openings that would be of interest to you. Would coffee at 4pm on Friday work for your schedule?"

You get the idea.

Always be aware of the power you hold. You can be useful to this person right now. Know your advantages and parlay them when it's appropriate.

Summary

1. The pro-active approach is the professional way to go about the business of job hunting

2. Pro-active job hunting goes from the industry to the niche industry to the company to your specific target group to your new boss

3. Create a spreadsheet to compare your target companies at a glance

4. Start with three target companies and build to 40 to ensure success

5. Contact your target company via direct contact with the hiring manager

6. Utilize Recruiter's tactics to find your new boss

7. When in contact with the hiring manager have them help you with your job hunt in exchange for information about job opportunities at other companies for him

In this chapter, the Predator is born. Own the premise and execute the mission.

CHAPTER 6
THE INTERVIEW

This may be the most important chapter in the book. You have worked hard to get yourself in front of the hiring manager with the job as the catch. Now, here you are.

I've been through hundreds of these interviews—on both sides of the table. The technique I'm going to give you comes from interviews I gave to top executives, as well as the way I was able to apply their best practices to being an interviewee myself.

Good interviews come from confidence, mutual respect, alertness and salesmanship. Reading and even re-reading this chapter, getting the format down pat, will help you to bring those qualities to your interviews.

In preparation for the interview it is vitally important to do your homework on the company. Hiring managers are impressed by how well you know their organization. As a job candidate, they know you are very likely looking at other companies, but it scores points with them if you give them the impression that their company is special. Showing your understanding of their company serves not only as a platform for deeper discussions but as a complement to their hard work and achievements within the market.

Be Prepared

- Review every possible question and have a good answer for each
- Research the Company—through their website, press releases, news articles, financials
- Bring downloaded copies of your research to the interview with highlighted sentences

Before you go into an interview you have to immerse yourself in preparation. Quiz yourself on what you might be asked, research the answer. Research the company, not just through their website but through third party sites as well. Print out articles, press releases, financials, white papers, industry ratings —and bring them with you, with key sentences highlighted. You won't use all this stuff, but have it all with you.

I have brought a file box with me to plenty of interviews. That image alone is impressive. Who brings a file box with them to an interview? How many other candidates will do that? Not too many. Before you even open your mouth you have sent a message. *I'm taking this interview seriously. I've done my homework. I am prepared.* Having all that material with you also helps put you in the right frame of mind.

The file box should be one of those clear ones with the handle. Those are sold in different sizes, so buy one just big enough to hold your folders. Be sure to have the file folders titled so you can find what you need right away. You want to avoid "dead-air time" while you finger through the folders. I usually look through my files while I'm talking so as not to break the conversational flow.

Put the file box on a chair next to you, not on the hiring manager's desk or the conference room table. You want the info available without having to bend out of sight to get a file from the floor, but you don't want it to be a distraction. Pop the lid open before the interview starts so you are ready. When you are looking for a document, get the folder and put it on the desk or conference table, then page through the contents until you find what you're looking for. Do this right in front of the interviewer. It's a nice image of you working, and breaks up the static setting of two people sitting upright and talking. This kind of movement is a good thing. If there is a white board in the room, take note of it, there will be opportunities to use it later in the interview.

If the image of a file box feels too old school for your style, or is inappropriate for the industry or company where you are interviewing—a digital archiving business, for instance — then by all means come to the interview with a laptop or tablet. Open your device and have the file on the company available. Make sure the open file has the name of the company on it. When you are discussing a particular document bring it up on your computer. You should have the parts of the document electronically highlighted so you can find what you are looking for quickly.

Feel free to rotate your device to show the interviewer what you are reading. Have them scroll to the top to see the title, date and byline of the document to verify its authenticity. Be sure your desk top is clear of personal files that the interviewer —or you—could inadvertently open.

Always come into an interview with a pad of paper (graph paper is best), a pen and a pencil. You will want to take down notes as well as diagram the workflow, placing the names of people in the network of the workflow. When you diagram the workflow materials do so clearly, making it easy to read and understand since you will be sharing this diagram with the interviewer from time to time, checking it for correctness.

Company Research

Let's discuss your research of the target company. I like to start with the company website because it shows you how they want the outside world to see them. Most companies spend a ton of money on their image and the website shows it—or should. Become familiar with what they want outsiders to know about them. You know this is where they show their best side, of course, their strengths and their achievements. So it's a good place to start.

The next thing to do is Google them. Read articles written about the company, both favorable and unfavorable. Print out articles that are particularly interesting.

The negative stuff is particularly useful. There will come a point in the interview where you start to interview them. You want to be able to have them talk about their weaknesses, and what they are doing to overcome them. Remember, their weakness is an opportunity to lay out steps for an improvement. If you can link yourself to such a plan you have a great chance of being hired. We will discuss this in greater length later in this chapter.

Check out their financial data via a finance or corporate information site of the kind sponsored by Yahoo, Google and MSN. If you find information that casts your target company in a bad economic light, don't be discouraged—there are tremendous opportunities in failing companies.

In 2001, after Silicon Valley's "Dot.Com Bust," I was asked to shift my negotiation skill set from our in-house executives to downsizing deals with partner companies and building leasing companies. I learned a lot, made more money and expanded my industry contacts—all good things especially in a down market. Making good money in a down market also allows you to buy stock, real estate and other investments at a discount. Down markets and failing companies provide huge opportunity for the development of new skills, strategic planning, using your creativity, testing new theories, etc. Find a way to get in.

Once you have collected all your data and have printed out what you think will be useful, highlight sentences or sections that remind you of key points. Note: these points can serve you both on defense and offense—you can use them to illustrate your answer to the hiring manager's question or as the premise for stating your own question.

This is where knowledge becomes power. Good information is like ammunition here—it will give you confidence and a sense of purpose when you walk into that interview.

Question List

Prepare a list of questions based on the material you've highlighted. Bring them in to the interview and place them on the conference table or interviewer's desk so they can be seen —a reference sheet for you, and an indicator of your preparation, seriousness, and level of interest in the company. Many times the interviewer will ask you to read some of your questions to gauge who he is talking to.

Title the paper, "Questions for _____ Corporation," so it's clear what it is to the interviewer at a glance. Their company name on the "question sheet" shows it is customized. This is a nice touch.

Interviewing Psychology

Take control of the interview early. Start with questions.

Say something like, "Before we get started I wanted to get some clarification on the open position. The job description says... (at this point you will very briefly give the job description, very briefly) ...is that correct, Mr. Johnson?" Or, if there isn't a formal job description, "I understand the position to be...is that correct Mr. Johnson?"

It's useful to clarify the actual position for which you are interviewing, but just as important is the impression it creates.

You are not entering the interview as a softy. You are here to conduct business.

Listen carefully to the interviewer's answer. It will frame your next question. Even if his answer contains no ambiguities you can summarize the answer and toss it back, saying, "So what you are saying Mr. Johnson, is...do I have it right?" His confirmation is what is known in sales as a "check close." You are both in agreement, you've closed the door on the topic, and now you are moving forward.

You are free to continue with your own questions if the hiring manager appears to be comfortable with your style, or you can turn it over to the interviewer—particularly if you sense he wants to move on. Your hand-off can be something like this:

"Thank you for the info, Mr. Johnson. I'll have more questions for you later but for now I'm sure you have a question or two for me." Try to end there with a small laugh, or at least a smile.

This opening exchange shows:

1. Cordiality, respect and grace under pressure

2. Communication on an equal footing

3. A business demeanor

If you have listened carefully to the hiring manager's answers you will have a pretty good sense of how he thinks and even feels. Facial expressions and body language will tell you a lot about how to deliver further answers and questions.

Not bad for the first few minutes of the interview.

The Interview Flow

As you can see, the idea is to make the interview interactive, working it until you are on equal footing with the interviewer —at the very least. Of course, you want the job but without gaining mutual respect it will be a one-way street, and certainly not to your advantage. You want to steer the interview into the job offer neighborhood, and this kind of interactive dialog is the foundation of your plan to get there.

Eventually you must yield the floor and allow the interviewer to ask his questions. The interview will be one-sided for a while, but remember, the interviewer will always provide an opportunity for you to ask questions or provide input so know you will get a chance to pursue your interactive interview tactics.

Later in this chapter I'll discuss the four different interview methods you can be exposed to.

Demeanor

Almost all of my colleagues agree that enthusiasm—or at least positivity—is the most important component of a successful interview. How can you display enthusiasm without coming off as fake? The keys are:

1. attentiveness

2. alertness

3. focus

Combined with an interactive exchange, these elements come down to listening carefully, finding a point for discussion, posing your question or comment, than listening carefully to the answer.

Don't let these mini-discussions go on very long: no long, drawn-out answers or complex multi-part questions. Keep it neat.

Present yourself as relaxed but aware. You don't want to come off as too intense and scare your interviewer, but if you appear too relaxed you will seem unengaged, too laid-back for the daily rigors of corporate life.

Listen carefully to what the interviewer is saying. Look for ambiguities, anything that is unclear. Take note of these, either mentally or on your notepad. At the first opportunity ask for clarification.

Say something like, "Excuse me Mr. Johnson, when you say the company is aggressive about marketing, do you mean the products or the company's image in the marketplace?" Or, "Are these targets to be reached in this quarter or the end of the fiscal year?" "Are the goals domestic or worldwide?"

Have these kinds of questions come out early so the interviewer knows you are listening, then back-off. You don't want to block the interviewer's flow.

Your First Interview Objective

Your first goal in the interview is to specifically identify the job description. Yes, it is spelled out on their website or job listing but it's safe to assume those are generic descriptions posted by HR. Until you talk with the manager that the position answers to, you will not know the exact job description or responsibilities. Now is your chance to find out. You should have lots of questions that end, "Mr. Johnson am I to understand that this is a specific responsibility of my position?" Every time the interviewer says, "Yes," make a note of it. You must know what they want of you, so you can determine:

1. what the position can do for your career

2. what your title should be

3. what is the proper compensation, based on the real title

If the posted position is for a software engineer but in the interview you realize your responsibilities include managing others with project responsibilities, you are interviewing for a team lead position, software engineer manager or project leader. Your title, compensation and career objectives are all affected by these responsibilities, so probe deeply into the real job description, not the posted one you thought you were interviewing for.

Your Second Interview Objective

Your other objective in the interview is to create a colleague-to-colleague relationship with the interviewer. In 3–5 years you will actually be his equal, so don't let yourself be intimidated by the interviewer or the process.

Remember, you were invited because they already see you as qualified. They are now looking to validate their selection and see if you fit into their group. The interview is now more about your soft skills then your technical skills: the interviewer will be looking at attributes such as character, passion, communication skills, team awareness, problem solving, leadership/initiative and work ethic. The company wants to know whether you are honest, trustworthy and driven to achieve their goals. Can you communicate effectively with managers, peers and subordinates? Are you a team player and a "fit" for their culture? These are vital questions for any employer.

My years of experience have shown me that being a good team member may be the soft skill the company is most interested in. I've seen highly qualified candidates get passed over because they didn't appear to be team players. I'd put trustworthiness right up there with team awareness. And work ethic is very important as well. They want to know that if something comes up at 5 p.m. you will stay to carry the project through—especially if it is customer related. Initiative and problem solving are important, but they are trumped by those other attributes.

Once, the VP of engineering asked me to find a software architect for one of his groups. I searched out a brilliant guy from a competitor company. Some of the other engineers knew of him and were surprised I was able to snag him. He was invited in for an interview on three separate occasions. In the end, though, they decided to pass on the candidate. I was shocked.

I knew it would be nearly impossible for me to find someone else with that kind of talent in our niche market. I immediately met with the VP of engineering and asked him what happened. He told me the candidate had an exceptional skill set, that even within the course of the interviews they learned something helpful about the technology. However, their sense was that he could be difficult to work with in a group environment, and that the group could be damaged by including him so they all agreed to pass on him.

What that meant was that the group would rather work harder to create solutions than have their dynamic compromised with the introduction of this superstar. Quite a statement, when you think about it: a world class company that relies on regular technological innovation passing on an engineering wizard to preserve their culture and team integrity. That's how important being a team player can be.

Creating an Outline of the Position

Once you have identified and checked the responsibilities of the job you're being interviewed for, begin to outline a schematic of your position—i.e., who you report to, who reports to you, what departments you will interact with to do your job. Then drill deeper: ask specifically who in those groups you will be interacting with. While discussing the workflow, refer to these people by name.

You are now in an interactive conversation with the hiring manager. You are gradually leaving the interview behind, and are beginning to do the job on a mock-planning level. Write this schematic down either on paper or a whiteboard so the manager can add or delete items. Your conversation should sound something like this, "So, Mr. Johnson, I'm here in this department. I'll interact with Bill Smith in Sales and Sue Peterson in Finance and sometimes with Betty Palmer in Legal, is that right?"

What you are doing is fleshing out the structure so that both of you are living the reality of you working in this capacity. You are creating a mental imprint together. It's mutual visualization.

Setting up the Second Interview

Mr. Johnson may make some adjustment and provide more information. Be alert. Figure out who is the most important person you will be interacting with, besides the hiring manager, then say, "What's the possibility of Ron Thomas joining our conversation?"

What you've done here is to set up the second interview. The hiring manager may call Ron Thomas in immediately or say, "Let's finish before I turn you over to Ron." Either way, a second interview is now on the table.

The New Plan

In this conversation with the hiring manager ask if he is happy with the current system of operation and the current workflow sequence. You pretty much can bet that he isn't. Remind him that your coming in may be a good opportunity to introduce something new. Almost every manager has spent some time thinking about a better way to do his job. You will simply be reminding him of his own new ideas for the department. Once you open the "new idea" box, sit back and let it sink in. You will almost be able to see the wheels turning in his mind. The psychological shift here is key—you have just connected yourself to something new.

It will be natural for the hiring manager to see you as an integral part in a bigger plan. In his thinking, you are now connected to his new reorganization plan. You've created even more value for yourself.

The dynamic you just created is a classic, three-step negotiation tactic:

• First, you overcome being submissive by interviewing the interviewer and getting clarifications on items of ambiguity.
• Second, you achieve a colleague-to-colleague relationship with the hiring manager by ironing out the details of your responsibilities in an interactive manner.
• Third, you put yourself on the same side of the table as your interviewer by interactively discussing your schematic of the position's workflow and duties, the departments and the people in those departments.

You are now both looking at the overall system and planning possible options for change. You and the hiring manager are working together, side by side, focused on a third element. You have raised your worth tremendously since you walked in the door. A second interview should be quickly forthcoming. Good work.

Workflow Schematic

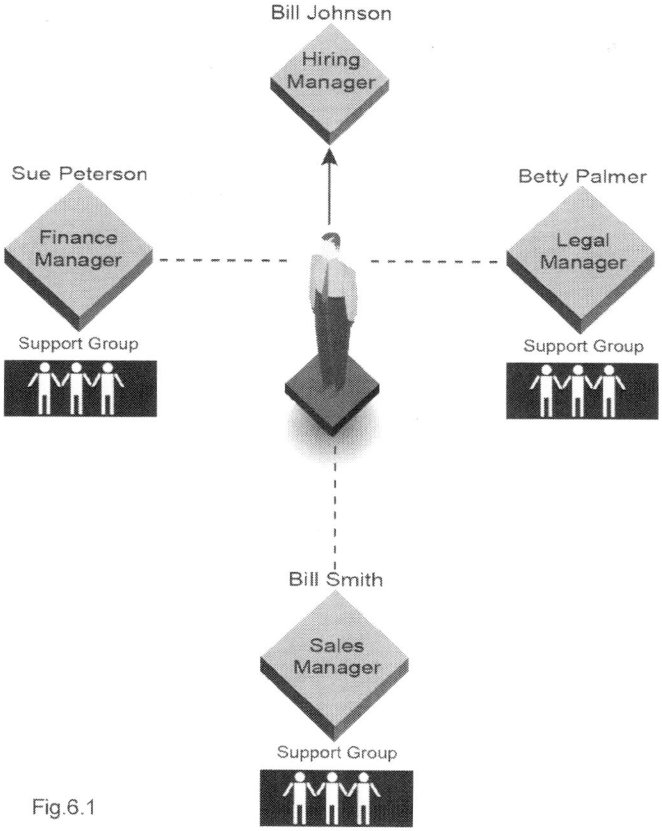

Bill Johnson
Hiring Manager

Sue Peterson
Finance Manager
Support Group

Betty Palmer
Legal Manager
Support Group

Bill Smith
Sales Manager
Support Group

Fig.6.1

The technique revealed in this chapter will, if nothing else, present you as a unique candidate. Who does an interview like this? Once you leave you will not be forgotten. This wasn't just an interview, it was an experience.

Many years ago I did an interview like this when I applied for a technical recruiter position at a top tier recruiting company with several branch offices. At the end of the interview the hiring manager offered me a position as the manager of a brand new branch. I came in to the interview for grunt work and walked out as a lieutenant.

If you handle the interview as outlined in this chapter your hiring manager will definitely be impressed, and in most cases work to find you a place in the company.

Interview Methods

Before we discuss interview questions you need to know about interview methods. There are four main interview types: the traditional interview, behavioral interview, case interview and stress interview. Of these, the traditional and behavioral methods are the most widely used. Of these two the traditional interview is still the method of choice but the behavioral interview is definitely gaining ground.

Before you enter into an interview, as part of your company research, you will need to use the networking techniques discussed in Chapter 4, Internet Job Hunting. By now, you have made a friend or two in your target company via Facebook, Twitter or LinkedIn. Ask them what kind of interview technique the company uses.

Keep in mind that in a down economy employers have a greater choice of talent to select from. Their qualifying standards will naturally be higher. They can experiment with interview techniques and make the entire process more challenging. If you expect and prepare for more difficult interview questions, the questions you actually get should be a walk in the park.

I will give you enough information to understand the method and know, in a general way, how to handle each type. Once your research uncovers the interview method(s) you are most likely to encounter, I suggest you seek out a book or two on that particular method. Each one is a study in itself. I have also suggested some reading that may help.

A word of caution here: some of these books list likely questions you'll be asked and tell you how best to answer them. While some answers can be clever, your goal is to develop critical thinking skills, strategy and tactics rather than memorize clever replies. Clever replies are useful as fallbacks when trying to answer a particularly difficult question, but a steady diet of them will give the hiring manager, candidate indigestion and keep you from receiving a job offer. Instead, learn the process and make yourself multi-dimensional.

Stress Interview

The Stress Interview is designed to knock you off your game. It's not so much the questions as the interviewer's challenging attitude. In keeping you off-balance the interviewer will attack your answers, personality, philosophy, etc, in an effort to expose you to a stressful situation for the purpose of finding out how you react to a difficult environment. As soon as you realize what's happening, understand that your best reaction is to be calm and let your mind focus on a balanced reply to a "mock" situation. It's a game—a nasty little game but a game nonetheless.

I was an in-house recruiter and had to interface with the VP of Sales. He came to us from a recently acquired competitor company and had a bad attitude about the corporate takeover of his company—a company where he was CEO. In our initial meeting he raked me over the coals to let me know he was in charge. My mental reaction to him was, "I'm not supporting him but rather his position." That way, his style of work was of no concern to me. I focused on what he listed as his needs to keep a successful sales force working at top level performance and did my very best to provide him with those requests. It wasn't long before he calmed down and became kinder.

At one point, he complimented me on the good work I was doing. I remained cordial, professional and most important focused on the task at hand. The lesson here is to handle the work and not the personality.

If you find yourself in a stress interview, turn it around by asking specific questions that will help you solve the mock problem. Don't get defensive. Maintain your composure at any cost.

There is plenty of information available on stress interviews on the web. I wouldn't spend money on a book on them—it's easy to understand, and a rare type of interview method. As such, I have no author or book recommendations for you here.

Case Interview

The Case Interview is designed primarily for management consultants and investment bankers at consulting companies like McKinsey, The Boston Consulting Group, Bain and Deloittle Consulting. An "Associate's" average salary at one of these firms is around $120,000 per year, and the majority of the candidates have an MBA. An Associate is expected to be on a team of 3-5 consultants, dispatched to a major division or subsidiary of a Fortune 500 company and told to "fix" it. Since their billing rate is high, they are expected to deliver solutions that are fact-based and easily understood by the client. Your interviewer is usually a working Consultant Team Lead or Manager. You will have to convince him you are worthy of being added to the team. Competency in working through complex issues is crucial, along with excellent communication of your solutions. Providing visuals like charts and diagrams are a big plus. You will get high marks in the interview if you deliver your answers in this manner.

The interview questions are of a problem-solving nature. You are expected to ask the interviewer questions to clarify and get more specifics about the case. Thinking out loud is good so the interviewer can determine how your mind processes the data and arrives at an answer. The process is more important than the answer, so show your work visually or at least verbally. You should never knowingly go into a case interview without proper preparation. Two authors I have found to be helpful in understanding case interviews are Marc P. Cosentino and Victor Cheng.

Behavioral Interview

Behavioral, situational or competency-based interviews—which, for simplicity, I will refer to as the behavioral interview—all function on the assumption that the best way to determine how you will behave in the future is to understand how you behaved in the past. The interviewer will ask you about your past achievements, failures and difficult situations with previous bosses, co-workers and customers, to name a few. The format is simple—a situation or problem will be stated and the interviewer will want to know what you did and how that turned out. The acronym for this is SAR—situation, action and result. I'd like to advise you to add one more step: moral. As in, "The moral of the story is…" In which case the acronym would be SARM.

The reason I'd add the "moral" component is that if the "result" of your story is less than perfect you want to find a way to end on a high note. By saying something simple like, "I learned a lot from that experience," (in a reflective tone) the interviewer will be compelled to ask a follow up question. This allows you to get a fresh opportunity to explain how this seemingly weak outcome has become a positive for you. This is a chance for you to come away with a win even with a poor outcome in your initial story.

An excellent way to prepare for the Behavioral Interview is to have a good understanding of what traits the job title requires or would be nice to have. Then, review your recent past work experience and find examples that address those traits as positively as possible. Write down these stories and study them. Remember, your "moral" card for iffy scenarios.

Since you've already thought about your answers, it should be easy for you to come up with a list of behavioral interview questions. Practice with a friend or family member. You'll be surprised at what can come out of an exchange like that—and it will only help to make you a stronger candidate.

If you haven't exhibited the positive traits necessary for this job in the workplace yet then review other recent experiences where you have—as a member of a volunteer organization, for instance, or a club, sports team, the military, etc. The interviewer will appreciate your candor about your relative lack of work experience and your attempt to provide a parallel example. "I can't recall a work place experience that matches your question," you might say, making it clear you are answering the question slightly differently, "but as a volunteer member of a local charitable group I encountered the kind of situation you have described. May I tell you what I did there and how it turned out?"

Some books that will help you answer behavioral interview questions are *Competency-Based Interviews,* by Robin Kessler and *High-Impact Interview Questions,* by Victoria A. Hoevemeyer.

Traditional Interview

The Traditional Interview is still the most common interview used, a combination of questions about your resumé and cover letter experiences along with basic qualifying questions such as: "Tell me about yourself. What are your strengths and weaknesses? What are your career goals? Why should we hire you? How are you in a pressure situation? What do you know about our company?"

With these kinds of questions the interviewer is trying to get insight into how much of a match you are for their company, and specifically their group. There is plenty of data both online and in print that address these types of questions. Some books to review on these kinds of interview questions are: *301 Smart Answers to Tough Interview Questions,* by Vicky Oliver and *101 Great Answers to the Toughest Interview Questions,* by Ronald W. Fry.

Traditional vs. Behavioral Interview – trends in interview methods

The Behavioral Interview has been around for almost 20 years. I actually remember when it was first starting to be used. Since then it's proved to be about five times more effective than the Traditional Interview in determining an employee's behavioral tendencies at work. You would think it would be the interview of choice for almost all employers by now. But the truth is, it's only used about 30% of the time. That begs the question, "Why?"

When it was first introduced at my company about 15 years ago all the managers were invited to attend a half-day workshop on how best to use the behavioral interview. Many of the managers didn't attend because they were too busy. Of those that did attend about half collected the workshop materials and left after the first break. You would think that something this important to the hiring process would have garnered more respect, or at least interest. It helps to understand the manager's response when you look at it from their point of view.

Managers do not really spend a lot of time interviewing candidates in comparison to the rest of their pressing duties. Second, they are lords of their group or department and feel they know what's best for their charges. One would be hard pressed to find a manager that doesn't think he couldn't sit down with a potential candidate and absolutely know, in a Q-and-A session, if the candidate could survive and thrive in his group.

So training in something that they do infrequently and that they are, in their opinion, very qualified to do, hold little to no interest for them. Believe me, this is universal.

As such, savvy employers have structured the interview process in a way that minimizes the hiring manager's exposure to the process. This is done through the use of a qualifying personality test and the test is laden with Behavioral Interview style questions. Something this successful in helping employers predict employee work behavior cannot be ignored.

The downside in all this is, the questions are tough and in many cases notch into the candidates dignity and self-respect causing highly qualified candidates to be insulted by the process. As such, many of these qualified candidates don't complete the process.

The de-humanization of the system needs to be calibrated to prevent the over-stepping of the use of technology and cost cutting methods to allow for humanity. In an employer's job market that effort holds little hope. As the wheel turns however, the mistakes of this kind of system will naturally move towards center.

We are in a tough economic climate but the predator must find a way to win. A solid solution for any interview methodology is good intel. Use the techniques described in Chapter 4 to befriend employees at your target companies. Talk to them, find out about the company culture, the manager you will be working for, the interview methods they use, the hiring process and company policies.

If the company is good for you but they use a tough personality test as their screening system, suck it up and get it done. Don't let yourself get caught up in the small stuff. On the other hand if the personality test is a prelude of things to come, move on. But make your decision on the basis of several data points, rather than just some challenging interviews.

Salary Questions

We don't have space in this book to go into all the different kinds of interview questions you're likely to be asked, and how I think you should answer them. If you feel you need that, the books I've recommended above should fit the bill. I will dive into the "Salary Question," however, because nothing I've read in other job hunting books hits the mark.

One essential thing to know about salary is that all corporations of significant size have a compensation band. That is, the HR department is conducting continual research on what fair market value is for every job title in the company. It's a full-time job for one person in many companies. They select one job title and create 3-4 levels for the job title based on experience. A software developer can be an entry level developer, junior level or senior level developer—each level holds a salary range. These numbers are designed to reflect what the regional market is for this position, and they are industry specific.

Corporations don't want to have their employees be the least monetarily compensated in the industry for a few reasons. One is that qualified candidates will not apply to their company. Believe me, the word gets around quickly about a company in the industry that pays at or below scale.

Two, they will become a "source" company for recruiters representing their industry competitors. If you are a recruiter for a competing company you know very well that underpaid employees will be happy to hear they are being sought after. Even if the employee doesn't leave they may use this interest from a competitor company to leverage their current position and compensation. Given the resources that go into training and retaining skilled employees, it's easy to see why employers are willing to pay someone a full-time salary to keep on top of the salary comp bands.

This is the real reason salary negotiations can be so tough. You are better off negotiating a higher classification of your title. In this way your hiring manager doesn't have to battle against the comp band to get you more money. However, if you ask to be classified as say, a senior software developer when the hiring manager already has two of them in his group with significantly more experience than you, he will risk upsetting the group balance.

I do not mean to be discouraging here—I simply want to give you the facts: corporate salaries are always being balanced within the small group you will work in, throughout the company across departments, industry-wide and regionally specific.

This is not to say that we are helpless. In Chapters 8 and 9 we will examine how we can get ourselves the best deal we can. As well, compensation and benefits, important as they are, should not be the only factor influencing your overall decision-making process If the people you are to work with seem like a good fit for your personality and skill set, and the company is on an upward ascent, there is more than one way to fix your compensation concerns. We will discuss this in depth later in the book.

Salary Discussion with the Hiring Manager

Now, let's look at this issue from a person-to-person point of view. By the time the salary question comes up you will have spent a fair amount of time with the hiring manager. You will know if they are the kind of person you could go out with after work or if they are strict about maintaining a professional distance between themselves and other employees. I mention that because when the hiring manager asks, "What are your salary expectations? Or, "What was your salary at your former employer?" you will have a few different ways to answer, depending on what kind of chemistry you have established with the hiring manager.

If you have gained a "buddy" type of relationship with them it will be easy for you to avoid directly answering. You can say something like:

"I'm glad you are bringing this up [and believe me you really are]. With the current economic climate it seems employers are adjusting their compensation bands hourly, (Pause) in the wrong direction." Some humor is not a bad idea but then move to a serious tone. "I'm looking to start at a salary that's fair for this position. What is your company's comp band for this title with my level of experience?"

You have just turned the question around. If they pause to think it over you can add, "Even a ballpark number would be helpful."

If they don't bite with this question then you can be more direct, and say, "The range of base salaries for this title, in this regional market is between _____ and _____. Is your company's comp band in this range?"

You should already know this range. If not, research it, www.salary.com is a good place to start.

Whatever the hiring manager says, your reply is, "Good."

This is not the time to discuss salary. You are just trying to get past by this inquiry, which actually means little or nothing at this time. There will be plenty of opportunity to discuss compensation later, after a job offer has been tendered. At that time you will have leverage because if they extend an offer you know they really want you. Right now they are just kicking the tires so don't knock yourself out of the running and let yourself be dragged into a pointless discussion. Don't give the interviewer an opportunity to disqualify you. A salary back-and-forth at this time will hurt you.

Even if afterwards you feel held to your verbal "OK," you can make up the difference through a signing bonus, a structured performance bonus, a good health benefits package, a substantial employers contribution to your retirement plan, stock options, gym membership, and the like. All this will be discussed in detail in Chapters 8 and 9. You have many cards you can play and it all plays better once they make a job offer.

Use their salary inquiry as an opportunity for you to gain knowledge about what they are willing to pay you. You are interviewing with other companies and although salary isn't your final consideration it's very important. So, you truly are happy when the subject comes up and you are even happier when they bring it up.

Remember, you have an agenda as well. At this juncture it's, "Find out what they are paying for this position."

If on the other hand you find that the hiring manager is hard-nosed, maintains a professional distance or is a no-nonsense personality then your approach needs to be different. Talking around the question or taking time to frame a complex answer may work against you so be direct.

"At my last job I made _____ per year but also had health coverage for my entire family with vision and dental, the employer's contribution to my 401K plan was 100% matching and I was given the use of a company car."

If this type of hiring manager asks you, "What is your salary expectation?"

You can say, "I'm looking to start at a salary that is fair for this position. The range of base salary for this title in this regional market is between _____ and _____. Is your company's comp band in this range?"

These kind of hiring managers appreciate directness if nothing else. It's a time saver. Remember, without an offer on the table all this is just talk. We will really go to work on the compensation piece when the time is right.

Review of Interview Flow

Since we have discussed many different points and types of interview approaches I'd like to help simplify what the interview flow should look like.

1. You start the interview with questions to clarify the job description so know what job you are interviewing for since the posted description may not be accurate.

2. If the interviewer seems comfortable with your style you can continue for a short while but at some time early in the interview you will gracefully hand the interview over to the interviewer.

3. You will have done your research and should have a good idea of what interview method you will be exposed to and be able to answer those types of questions.

4. You will have time at the end to ask your questions and work the interview to your advantage. At that time, use the outline of the job position, the interaction with other managers, your attempt to secure a second interview and your idea for making you part of a new plan to the hiring manager.

Summary

We have covered a lot of ground in this chapter. Let's review.

1. You take control of the interview early by asking questions about the job description

2. After your initial questions are answered, you cordially and gracefully hand over the interview to the hiring manager

3. You may ask a question or two for clarification just to let the interviewer know you are listening but for the most part you let the interviewer direct the interview

4.   You will have done research mainly through company contacts that you have made via Facebook, Twitter, LinkedIn, etc., to determine what kind of interview method you will be exposed to

5.   There will always be an opportunity to ask your questions so bring your file box/electronic tablet/laptop and your customized question sheet for this company

6.   Be prepared with a comprehensive array of company data this will serve you in both answering and asking questions

7.   Read the interviewer's facial expression and body language in addition to assessing their thinking to get a clue as to how to ask and answer questions

8.   Work to develop a colleague-to-colleague relationship with the interviewer

9.   When the time is right begin to create an outline of your position including the other groups/departments you will interface with—launch a discussion with the hiring manager on the subject

10. Be sure to get the names of the other people your job duties cause you to work with and refer to those interactions using the names of those people

11. In the discussion with the hiring manager about your day-to-day responsibilities find who the second most important person is and ask for that person to join your current discussion. This is a setup for a second interview

12. Ask the hiring manager if he is satisfied with how the current system is working

13. Introduce the idea that with your hiring this may be just the right time to change the current system

I consider this chapter the brains of the book. It would serve you well to re-read it a few times until you can simply look at the sub-headers I've labeled throughout and know the content. This chapter contains the blueprint for conducting the best interview you have ever done—Own it.

CHAPTER 7
EXTRAS: PHONE SCREEN
SECOND INTERVIEW—BACKGROUND CHECK

As you've learned, a lot goes into the job hunt. We've collected a number of other relevant items the Job Hunter needs to know into this chapter.

Phone Screen

Companies don't always do a phone screen to evaluate candidates, but if you are called be relaxed and positive. You need to know who the interviewer is—what is their role in the hiring process? Are they the hiring manager, an HR representative, a support person for the hiring manager, or someone else? Ask the interviewer their title. That may clear it up immediately. If not, ask directly where they fit in the hiring process. And if they are not part of the hiring process then ask who directed them to call you. This information will help you to frame your answers.

If you are applying for a technical position and your phone screener is from the specific group you wish to join, your answers of course, can be of a technical nature. If the screener is from another department, ask him or her what their relationship is with your group. Again, this will help you to frame your answers.

Remember, while you can provide technical answers to a screener from the group, your answers need to be more general with someone from HR, and you may have to explain the more technical points. Respond to an HR screener as if you were at a social event talking to someone with little or no knowledge of what you do for a living.

Don't be shy about periodically asking the screener if they understand what you just said. If they are going to summarize the call for someone else they need to have a general understanding of what you're telling them. This approach also helps you reveal subjective attributes like kindness and patience. The phone screener may convey that to their supervisor; if not, they will at least have a more positive impression of you, and you will have made another friend in your industry. You can't fully measure the value of friendly interactions, but they're certainly better than making an enemy.

I can't emphasize enough the value of being thought of as a team player. I have been in discussions with accomplished technical groups after an interview with an outstanding talent and seen the members of the group downgrade a brilliant candidate because they got the impression his or her personality was not a fit for their group culture.

Are you one of those people? If so, you will need to find a way to smooth out your rough edges or be prepared to live with rejection even if your experience and skills are exceptional.

This is a tricky business, of course, and there is a fine line between trying to become someone you are not and simply softening your persona. You may want to get an outside critique on this from people whose objective opinion you trust. It's worth the expenditure of time and energy to find out if you come across as unfriendly, arrogant, rough around the edges or unsociable. It may be the reason you are getting few or no job offers. Usually, the correcting of those types of personality quirks takes a little bit of attention to the manner in which you ask and answer questions. A slight adjustment like this is a small price to pay for getting a job offer.

Second Interview

If you've gotten a second interview, congratulations! But don't assume you come to a second interview with any good graces. Treat your second interview like the first. Why?

While you created a strong enough relationship with the hiring manager to have a second interview, this person doesn't know you and you don't know them. They may be in sync with the hiring manager, they may want to be more independent. Until you know whether the OK from the hiring manager is good for you, treat the second interview in a very professional manner.

The interviewer will have something they want to know right from the start. When you sense their questions are winding down, be pro-active. Say something like, "Bill Johnson (the hiring manager) outlined my job responsibilities. Here is a list of them."

Start to read them, but pause between points so the interviewer has a chance to make a comment. This will be very informative. You will learn whether your interviewer sees your position the same way as the hiring manager or not. If he does, ask for his input. If he sees the job differently, ask him, "What do you see the job as being?" Then adjust the responsibilities and reports on the list in line with the interviewer's comments and changes.

By now you should be where you were with the hiring manager: discussing the workflow of the position and everyone else in the picture. Again, you should find yourself planning the future of your position, not interviewing. Re-introduce the possibility of using your hiring as an opportunity for change. Remember, this ties you to a bigger picture and creates excitement. You have subtly taken some pressure off yourself by becoming part of a larger dynamic. Way to go.

The interview dynamic we've laid out is probably new for you. If so, it will take some courage to carry out. The main premise is this: you've researched the job well, and now you know it. You should comfortably be able to plan ways of actually doing the job with your boss, and even restructuring the work group, if you have the chance—and here it is. It's a rare opportunity to sit and plan this out. Go for it.

This kind of initiative and forward thinking reflects well on you. But keep in mind that it's not just theater—you really are doing important work to make your job as rewarding as it can be when you get it. That should help make this approach feel important.

Now, if you aren't a very outspoken person it's always good to have some simple questions prepared to help you warm up to the task.

Example:

- Is this a new position or did someone just leave?
- How long has the position been open?
- Does this position report to you?
- How long have you worked for XYZ Inc?

Create lots of questions like these. Some may be used to break the ice, others to bridge the gap between subjects. These are all a part of coming into the interview prepared. Load up your tool box. Remember, you are here to capture the job. Do your homework and be prepared.

Even more important is having the right mindset. This is the time to repeat the mantra, "Live the dignity of your potential, now."

Envision yourself as being asked by the interviewer, "If you were in my position what would you do to make this group better?"

Maybe the first thing you'd do is try to understand the group's workflow or the interaction between this group and other groups. When you have enough information then you can begin to suggest solutions or efficiencies. Initially, start with a soft approach.

"Have you tried to combine the production portion of your group with engineering thereby creating a junction point or translator between the two groups? This go-between would be someone that knows the working of both groups and has the communication skills and demeanor to clearly convey the info in a smooth and productive manner. What do you think?"

(Note how this sample suggestion is phrased in the form of a question. They will appreciate your having an informed, independent opinion, but you don't want to appear brash, or like you know their business better than they do. Especially for a job applicant, confidence and humility play well together.)

Listen closely to the interviewers' reply. The tone of the answer or the avoidance of a topic may reveal an important, underlying issue here. This is where your awareness and focus pay off. Dig deeper if you sense you are hitting on something. If you are lucky enough to sniff out a key component adversely affecting the workings of this group, you are in a real position of power.

You will naturally find your curiosity is aroused. You will want to know more about this little glitch, so ask the obvious questions. Be sensitive here, however. You need to tread carefully because you may be near a nerve.

Once you have gotten all the data you can about the situation, without being indiscreet, ask for permission to proceed.

"Is it OK for me to suggest something about this?"

These are your soft skills at work. You are showing compassion, consideration of the delicate nature of the subject matter and respect for the interviewer. It's not unlikely to realize you don't have enough experience to provide a valid solution, of course, but you can offer to help:

"I'd be happy to help you research anything you think would be helpful to solve this issue."

Remember that people don't always need solutions to difficult problems. Sometimes, they just want a nonjudgmental listener.

The end result is that with each in-depth exchange you continue to add value as a candidate. You are making it hard for them to discount you for the position. This is how you win the job.

Background Check

You would be hard pressed to find a corporate employer that does not perform a background check on a new hire. Interviews are self-validating—interviewers can see for themselves whether the candidate is confident, knowledgeable and smart. But to get corroborating data on what kind of an employee the person is over the long term, the employer relies on 3rd party verification from references, as well as a background check for factual confirmation of submitted resumé info.

Statistics indicate that more than 30% of job candidates lie on their job applications. Even though the lies may be of a minor nature, and those applications are primarily for lower echelon jobs, the number is significant enough to warrant factual confirmation of the data submitted by candidates for all positions.

Regardless, it would be negligent for an employer to bring a new hire into their company family without first having them checked out. And the greater the level of security needed to protect the company and its customers, the deeper the background check.

Dates of previous employment, title held and duties performed are commonly verified in background checks. So is education at the school listed, dates attended and degree(s) received. Criminal checks are standard as well. Investigators check federal, state and county records, usually going back 7 years, though some employers ask for more.

This search for the most part is for criminal convictions. However, if your new job requires you to handle or account for money, your employer may want to add a credit check to all the previously mentioned background checks. They want to see if you are a good custodian of your own finances and that you are not in deep financial trouble while having access to company funds.

Some companies contract with federal or state governments. If so, you may find your employer is required under contract to conduct even deeper checks. Investigators may want to interview your friends, family, neighbors and even previous co-workers.

If you are an executive and have been in the industry for some time your employer may investigate your financial holdings as well, in addition to other business partnerships or corporations you or your family may be invested in or have obligations to. The higher the position you are applying for, the more employers will want to know what and where your true motivations are. Conflict of interest is a real concern.

These background checks are expanding into a candidate's digital presence, as well. This means that investigators check social and professional networks, personal blogs and websites to get an idea of what you are posting. They are looking for anything that may compromise or embarrass their company, including your Facebook, Twitter, LinkedIn, Flickr, YouTube and Amazon activity.

The accuracy of background checks, in general, isn't as great as one might think. I've read figures as low as 60%. The reasons for that inaccuracy can range from a mistaken investigation of someone else with a similar name to the sheer amount of cumulative data. The FBI, for instance, has to collect vast amounts of data from different states and counties on a daily basis.

That can lead to sloppy or scattershot fact-checking. Criminal checks are not done by someone calling up a law enforcement agency and going over detailed info of the candidate to insure they are investigating the correct person. Investigators simply run an electronic search using a Web-based service and sees what comes up.

Seeing as you are likely to be the target of just such an investigation, it's good to ask, "What can I do to protect myself?" You may want to see what comes up on these searches, too."

Most of the top-tier, online search companies like US Search, PeopleFinders and Intelius have a service that allows you to run a search on yourself for a nominal fee. This will give you an idea of what your employer might see.

One on-line search firm, TrueRep goes a step further. They actually rate you by issuing you a "reputation score". The thing I found most interesting is that through this service you can make notations about questionable items on your search. This could be very important since most employers will not tell you why you were rejected for employment at their company. So, if your social media activity, driving record or frequent residence relocation seems odd, you can give yourself a fighting chance by commenting or explaining the event.

Most companies will use background services that are more sophisticated than these on-line search companies but it's in your best interest to search your own information through them, get clear on possible red flags and, if possible, explain questionable data, at least while you are job hunting.

Summary

1. In phone screen interviews, always know who you are talking to and where they are in the hiring process—this will help you frame your answers

2. Be sure to display soft skills like kindness and patience during the phone screen

3. In the second interview list your job duties per the hiring manager's interview to reconcile them with the way the 2nd interviewer sees your duties

4. Once you know what the 2nd interviewer is looking for steer the interview to a schematic of the workflow and deliver a vision of possibilities for the best use of your talent, much as you did with the hiring manager

5. Through an interactive discussion of the workflow and group dynamic probe the second interviewer to understand issues or concerns that hinder best practices

6. Use the info uncovered in the 2nd Interview to frame your problem-solving suggestions, or, if the problem is beyond your capabilities to solve, offer your assistance to help research solutions

7. The greater the level of security needed to protect the company and their customers the deeper the background check

8. Social and professional networks, personal blogs and websites are now targeted on most background checks

9. Do an online background check on yourself before you go out job hunting

We covered a lot of ground in this chapter. I think the most potentially hazardous area we discussed is the background check—particularly those that let background investigators look into your social networks. These are places where your guard is down. You let loose with friends and associates on Facebook and Twitter, and you might keep a blog about an eccentric or edgy interest. Unfortunately, this digital age currently doesn't yet call foul against an employer that wants to push background checks to the max. All we can do is be careful about what we post and engage protection options and services to defend against this kind of search. I hope I've helped to make you more aware of this and given you some tools you can use in your own defense.

CHAPTER 8
THE OFFER AND YOUR COUNTER OFFER

The offer letter is the first concrete signal an employer really wants you—take it seriously. This is where you have been working to be. However, you should also realize that the offer letter is a form letter generated by HR, based on hundreds of previous new hires. It's not tailored to you and likely to be about 80% accurate.

The more senior the position, such as manager or VP level, the less accurate the letter will be. Obviously, the level of latitude required of a VP, a senior grade officer of the company, is different than a team member of a small production group. The long and short of it is that with 80% accuracy, there is 20% left for you to adjust.

Let's look at the main components contained in the offer letter to see what we can revise.

Job Title

The first component of the offer letter is the job title. The job title must accurately match the job responsibilities you were able to define from your interviews. HR wants the job title to describe the lowest end of the compensation band for obvious financial reasons. For instance, if you are hired as a junior software developer but some of your responsibilities are those of a QA (quality assurance) Engineer, HR may say, "We are going to title you as a QA Engineer, initially."

This is not good for you. QA engineer is not the correct title for your position, nor will it give you the correct pay scale. Every company has what is known as a "comp band" (compensation band) for every single title. As I have mentioned in Chapter 6 when I discussed interviews, these bands are closely monitored across your industry. In large companies there are experts that do nothing but comp band analysis by industry and region. So right from the start your title must reflect your duties.

This is also important from a career perspective. It's better to start your career as a level 1 software developer than as a QA engineer. Being a software developer could essentially put you ahead by 1-2 years of promotions, and place you in a position to make team lead or manager that much faster.

I was an inside recruiter at a software development company and had located an excellent senior software engineer with lots of management experience. He was qualified to be a Director level candidate and could have easily stepped up to VP level in a year or two. However, this candidate was finishing a project at another company and could not join us full-time for about another month.

My company needed his technical know-how right away and was willing to bring him on immediately as a consultant to have him help us with an engineering trouble spot. They said that after he was in there and had helped with the problem they would work through the details of his title and compensation.

When I conveyed that to him he thought about it for a while. "It's very important how someone gets introduced to the company," he said when he got back to me. "It shapes the group structure. I want to wait until we can sit down and iron out all the issues of my hire."

He was concerned that the engineers he'd be working with as he helped solve our technical problem would harbor some resentment toward him, or show him a lack of respect, once he got promoted from consultant to Director.

He came on board at a later date as Director of Engineering and was very well received. He ended up making excellent contributions to the group. His decision to come in as Director instead of as a consultant was absolutely correct. I knew it at the time, too, but as an agent for my company I had to give it a shot.

Compensation

The next component of interest in the Offer Letter will be compensation. Compensation is a product of the company's comp band so there is little latitude here. Keep in mind, however, that comp bands are just that—bands. They have a range. It may be difficult finding out this range. Try talking to any friends you have made in the company using the social or professional internet network techniques we discussed in Chapter 4, and/or researching the matter yourself. In either case, do your homework to make sure that your compensation is commensurate with your title and level of experience in your industry and region. There are websites like salary.com that are focused on just this area. Check these kinds of sites regularly— once a quarter—even after you are employed. You should always know what you are worth in the market, right now. That kind of situational awareness is key for the predator.

I was doing outside recruiting: several companies would ask me to find qualified candidates for their key openings. One company was just starting a big growth campaign so they asked me to consider recruiting for their positions exclusively. This meant I would work on their premises and get paid on an hourly basis. This is called inside or in-house recruiting. This was outside my experience at this point. After an hour and a half of discussing my job responsibilities we got to the compensation. They asked me, "What is your rate?" In other words, "what do you want to get paid per hour to fulfill these job responsibilities?"

I thought $60 per hour might be a good number to start with, but I didn't say that. The truth was that I hadn't done my homework; I didn't know what I was worth. Instead, I turned it around and said, "We've been discussing this position and my qualifications for over an hour. I think you have a better idea of what I'm worth to you than I do."

There was a long pause in which I just looked at the hiring manager and said nothing. This is an effective negotiation technique: put something on the table, do not speak, wait as long as you have to for a reply. You've made an offer, you need an answer. If you say something—literally anything at all—you will undermine your own credibility. At the very least you will be qualifying your own offer; at worst you will seem willing to adjust your offer. Don't bid against yourself—make an offer and wait for an answer. Period.

Finally, the hiring manager said, "How's $80 per hour?" I was very happy inside, of course, but didn't show it. And while I thought it was a good number, without research, I wasn't sure. I didn't really know what I was worth.

I said, "I'm not sure if 80 is too much or not enough. Why don't we try it for say, three months and see where we are then?"

In other words, I'll agree to $80 an hour on a 90-day basis, but then we'll write a new contract. At the end of 90 days, I asked for a raise and got it. By the end of 9 months, I was getting paid $120 an hour. At that time I was asked to be the project lead, but I may have gotten it quicker if I had known what I was worth in the beginning.

All my success at that position came from my high levels of productivity. If you are very self-motivated, you need short-term contracts so you can prove to your employer how valuable you can be. At the end of each contract, mutual agreement on a raise is easy.

Once you have a good sense of what your compensation should be, look at what the offer letter says. If your research shows the offer to be on the low end you need to talk this over —but not with HR.

By now, you have a good idea of who wants you in the company, and who was instrumental in generating the offer. If there is any doubt about this, the hiring manager is the most likely suspect. This person—the hiring manager or whoever else you think it is—is where you need to start the conversation about upgrading your compensation. Begin by stating facts. "Mr. Johnson, I've reviewed three salary-related websites (you should name them), and the range for someone with my title and experience is between _____ and _____ per year. Here's a copy of my offer letter; as you can see the amount is _____. That is at the low end for this industry and region."

This may serve to clear things up immediately. The hiring manager may not even know what HR entered for your compensation. On seeing this he or she may simply say, "Sorry about that. Let me take care of this."

However, if the hiring manager is aware of the compensation and feels that it is the correct figure, then you have some work to do.

Start that conversation with all the reasons that you want to work for the company. Then ask the hiring manager why he or she selected you for the job over the other candidates. This should serve to remind him or her of what it would mean to have you on board. If you recall anything particularly favorable about you doing the job that he or she said during the interview, reiterate it. You are attempting to show all your value-added features. Then just say outright, "Mr. Johnson, I'd be a lot happier if I could get _____." State your number here and make sure it's in the range of your research. Then, while looking directly at the hiring manager ask, "What can we do?"

Then don't say another word. You have just put a counter offer on the table, let it be addressed.

The way you phrased your question turns it into a problem-solving exercise, so if it's not readily agreed to, you have opened the door for a back and forth discussion.

If the hiring manager comes back with a decent upgrade, take it. It's not a good thing to try and play hardball or squeeze your new boss. After all, you will be working with this person, and you don't want to try his or her patience before you are even hired.

On the other end of the spectrum, if there is no give whatsoever then you will have to think it over. You should say that. "Well, Mr. Johnson, thanks for hearing me out on this. I'd like to think this over some more. Can we talk tomorrow?"

You will want to go home and lay out the whole offer and what you feel about the job and the company. Is it a good fit for your skill set and personality? Does it provide a good chance for advancement, working in a positive environment with good people? If your other options are slim don't throw all that away because of a salary offer that's a bit low.

I have to say that compensation is not the most important item in the decision-making process when it comes to accepting a job offer. If it's a corporate environment, the comp band is probably very close to what you might get somewhere else. In the worst case, you take the job but continue to job hunt. Try to be objective here. Don't let your emotions run the show. Talk it over with a friend or family member whose sound judgment you trust.

Performance Bonus

I love the idea of a performance bonus because it establishes a platform for more pay, based on merit. Merit-based systems are the real essences of business.

A performance bonus allows you to show your employer what you can do with the right incentives. It also gives you a concrete reason to go above and beyond. It's absolutely a win-win situation. From a psychological perspective you are more inclined to take ownership under this kind of system. As a result, you become more attentive to the comings and goings in your group, department, company and industry. You raise your level of awareness, honing the instincts of the predator. That is always a good thing, and in this case it will lead to promotions or spin off into an independent position such as advisor, consultant, expert in a niche market, etc. You will learn so much more about your job with a performance-based bonus in place.

Most career experts feel the performance bonus is only for direct, revenue-generating positions, e.g. sales, professional services, customer service, etc. I think a performance bonus can be applied in any group in the corporation. There isn't a group/department in the company that doesn't have performance criteria, some level of deliverables. Take a moment and look at your current job. I'm sure you can list several job objectives that are measurable and thereby identified as "performance evaluators," subject for discussion between you and your immediate supervisor in a performance review.

So give some thought to what a performance bonus structure would be for your current position, then think what it could look like for the position you are seeking. Create two performance structures, one that is very complex and another that's very simple. You are then prepared to deliver a custom structure that falls between these two structures depending on the boundaries of the hiring manager. You have done lots of research about your new company and its industry. Use this info to help create an effective performance bonus.

Note that the performance bonus isn't always a dollar amount. It can be stock options, or even privileges, like a seat within higher-level meetings that affect the decision-making process in your department or the use of a company car.

This kind of approach will again highlight your ability to think outside the box. If you can do this to get the best situation for yourself, you can do it for the group and the company. Later in the book we will discuss Strategy Skills Development. This is a natural outgrowth of the performance bonus mindset. This is the art of business: creating options in such a way that you generate a real business advantage in an increasingly competitive environment.

Stock Options

Stock options are part of almost every job offer. The company wants you to feel that you have some level of ownership. The options are designed to yield dividends at a later date. In this way there is an incentive for you to stay with the company at least until your stock options are vested or reach a level of negotiable maturity. Until the stock options are vested they have no market value.

There are two negotiable components in the stock piece. First, there is the amount of stock that is offered—the number of shares—and second, the length of time in which the stock is vested.

With the amount of stock offered, a good rule of thumb is to counter the number of stock options offered by 10-20%. Regarding shortening the length of time in which the options vest, good luck—that's a tough sell.

Options are vested usually between six months and two years depending on company policy, which is strictly upheld. Changing the vesting period could open up this can of worms because it can affect others and cause a domino effect. You will have more latitude if you are coming on board as an executive since job offers for senior positions are expected to have a give-and-take dialogue. If you decide to counter the vesting period, counter it only by a small amount. If the current vesting period is one year, counter with nine months. If you get a lot of pushback, drop it. The advantage you are fighting to get will not be worth the negative impression you are creating.

To change the vesting period in a company takes sign-off from more then just the HR manager. It's conceivable that finance, legal and elements of senior management could be involved, not to mention the board of directors. Stock options and their valuation is a big thing, and it's not a good idea to have all those folks looking at you wondering why you want to rock the boat before you have even been hired.

However, if you are coming on for a short project due to your strong level of expertise in a particular area and the stock options will vest long after you have moved on, it makes sense to attempt to shorten the vesting period, even if it means rocking the boat. In fact, this kind of one-off situation is actually a good opportunity to work your vesting period into a performance bonus.

Let's say the employer is looking for a turnaround project manager—that is, someone brought in exclusively to turn a so-so department into a profit center—and that project manager is you. Something like this is usually short-term. Once done, neither you nor the company may want to continue together.

Now, once the conversion has been made the company will not have realized the profits from those changes yet. So you can take a "bonus compensation" for a job well done, under budget and under time, in the form of vested stock options. This would comprise a nice performance bonus in addition to your monetary compensation.

This scenario affords you the opportunity to get a front-end payment—your compensation—and a back-end payment—the stock. Of course, this is something to be set up before you accept the job. If you are the expert they think you are you will already know how long and how much money it will take to complete the project. Create an incremental bonus structure that delivers both monetary and stock options at the completion of agreed-upon milestones.

Say the project to turn around a particular department is slated for completion in one year and is budgeted for $1.8 million. After close review, you think you can do it faster and for less money. You could structure an agreement that allows you to get a certain amount of vested stock for every month under one year. Remember to prorate by the day in such a deal.

For the budget amount you can structure an agreement that let's you get, say, 30% of every dollar under that $1.8 million. This is just a sample bonus structure. Think about it, use your creativity and produce some sample bonus structures of your own.

Side-bar: Regarding Career Tracks

A word of caution here. If you do a good job and bring the project in under time and budget, the company may be so impressed that they will offer you an ongoing position in that department. At this point you will need to truthfully evaluate your skills and demeanor. Could you be happy as that department head? Does that fit your personality, style and work tempo?

It's tempting, but you may be a turnaround person, a fixer, at heart. There is a certain tempo to this job and it may not be easy for you to step into a slower, long-term pace. Be careful not to sell yourself out and go against your own nature.

I was recruiting for a VP level software engineer when I came across a perfect match. He was in a startup company, and had helped take it from a handful of people to a company of about 40 employees strong. He was ready to move on. He asked how big my company was. I told him we were at 175 and growing.

He said, "You are too big. I'm an early stage guy."

He had the skill set to do the job but he knew his personality would not be a fit for our company culture. Even though, a year from now we would be a company of 700 and he could be a key member of that growth, he knew this wasn't a position for him. He was more comfortable running around wearing many hats and shaping the new company with a small group. The company environment is different, the tempo is different and the exchange between co-workers is different. He already knew he would not be a happy camper in anything other than an early-stage startup. Personally, I really admired this guy for knowing himself and sticking to his guns. People like him are known as "architects." He knew many other creators in our industry and that info was valuable to me as a recruiter, so I ended up using him as a resource from time to time.

Health Plan

In the offer letter the company health plan is mentioned but not outlined. You need to know if the plan includes dental and vision and if the plan is just for you or includes your dependants. Is the plan valid worldwide or only locally? Are you covered on vacation out of the country? You may not be able to do much in this area since the plan is usually a company-wide program but you still need to ask the questions to understand the value of the entire offer. Knowing the details allows you to measure the offer properly.

These plans often have different options. You need to collect information for each option, take that info home and seriously research it. If you have made friends in the company using your social and professional internet networks, communicate with them and see what they have to say. If they have worked for the company for any length of time they will know about the strengths and short comings of each of the health plans offered. If they don't seem to know much about it, maybe because they are young, don't have a family and haven't really used the plan, then ask them if they are acquainted with someone that might know more about the health plans. Now that you have a job offer they should be freer with their internal contacts. Use everything you have available to you.

401K

Again, while the rules for the company's 401K plan are derived from state laws and company policy, you should at least know the percent of the employer's contribution. There is a big difference in this area. I've seen the employer contribution range from 2% to 100%. When you are looking at two nearly identical offers this can make a difference. If they have other retirement options, as with the health plan dig into it. Take home the materials, read them carefully, do Google searches and talk to your in-company contacts.

Summary

1. The Offer Letter is concrete proof that the company wants you, but the first rendition of the offer is usually only 80% accurate

2. You will need to study the offer closely to fill in what's missing or not complete

3. Start your research with the Job Title—make sure it matches what the hiring manager has said and that the title is the highest level of the job description possible for your duties and experience

4. Compensation is somewhat fixed through the compensation band but even in these bands there are ranges; ideally you want to be in the high end of that range

5. Compensation is not the most important factor in the decision making process to accept or reject the job

6. The performance bonus could be the best tool you have for increasing your compensation and increasing productivity, thereby creating a win-win situation

7. Stock Options can be tricky. Re-read this section before you make a counter offer. Remember, a 10-20% increase is a good rule of thumb

8. With both Health and Retirement Plans, try to get info from a few data points, particularly people you can talk to within the company; folks that have really used the plans will be your best source of useful information

We have closely examined the fine points of common items found in the offer letter and have seen some solid avenues for creating a basis for a counter offer, as well as how to clarify and restructure a better offer. The end result is that you will be working at a company you tracked down through your predator research skills—and now you are ready to become a star by launching a powerfully successful career. Good work!

CHAPTER 9
OFFER LETTER—EXECUTIVE VERSION

Before you skip over this chapter, if you're not an executive candidate, you should know that I'm going to cover several points regarding your offer letter that are not exclusive to executives. Items such as sign-on bonus, gym membership and relocation assistance, could be part of a non-executive offer letter also. I suggest you go through this chapter and see what else could be in your offer. Just because it isn't there doesn't mean you can't ask for it.

Once when I was doing in-house recruiting I brought in a junior level software developer. The hiring manager liked him and made him an offer on the first interview. I overheard the hiring manager talking to HR about writing the offer, asking if a gym membership could be included in this candidates offer letter. HR didn't have any rules against it and wrote it in. Once I found that out, I asked the HR Manager if he could get me a gym membership as well. "Sure," he said, and even though I was a contractor and not an employee, I got one as well. You don't know until you ask.

As an Executive, your offer letter will be more customized. The standard compensation items will be there but so will some perks. You will probably have discussed these things in a general way in talking with HR or a recruiter; now it's time to spell them out in detail and make them part of the offer letter. Read the previous chapter if you haven't done so, since the material in that chapter covered the fundamentals for the executive cover letter.

Privileges

Every company provides some kind of additional privileges for their executives. Look for them in your offer letter. If you don't see them ask about them. These can range from the key to the executive bathroom, to use of the company jet. Mostly they consist of a smart phone, a company car, a company credit card, deluxe travel arrangements and lodging for business trips, or membership to a local country club or a deluxe gym or spa.

Decision-Making Process

As an executive you must be part of the decision-making process. Make sure this is clearly stated in your offer letter. From my perspective, I don't know how any executive can be expected to run his or her department without having some participation in the decision-making process.

As an officer of the company you need to take ownership of your responsibilities. If you aren't getting your message across in the E-Staff (Executive Staff) meetings then you will need to arrange one-on-one meetings with Senior Management. After having a few of these meetings, senior management will get the point. They will begin to support you regarding E-staff meeting so they don't have to meet with you one-on-one afterwards. Ideally they will want to support you because they like your ideas and go-get-'em attitude.

If you have had success with your one-on-one meetings, work to continue them. Getting support for your ideas doesn't always happen in E-staff meetings due to competition from other executives fighting for the same pot of money. Any time you get traction with senior management, do what you can to keep that door open. We all know growing a successful department takes a fine blend of sound business practices and good, old fashioned politics.

E-Staff

As an executive you should be allowed to participate in the E-Staff meetings. Make sure you are, and have it stated in your offer letter. The E-Staff and the Board of Directors is where all major decisions play out. You need to be a part of that process.

You must understand that it's in the E-staff meetings where you will begin to make your mark. You are not here to be a spectator. You are on the team and must make a contribution. That's your first goal. I'll say more about this in Chapter 12— Strategic Skills Development—but for now, you need to know that E-staff meetings will be your playground. You will test well thought out ideas here. They won't all meet with success, of course. That is when you go back to the drawing board and build a better mouse trap.

Your second goal will be to rise beyond the level of "contributor," to innovator—a pragmatic innovator. You aren't aiming at just making the lineup, you want to bat cleanup, and then be named MVP. If you play with the goal of survival— not to lose—you won't win. You will wash out.

Here's where you need to plan your success. If I have you excited right now, jump to Chapter 12 and give it cursory review. It's a major cornerstone of building the predator.

Gym Membership

There is a veritable cornucopia of minor privileges you will inherit as a new executive member of the company. A gym membership is a good one. Ask for it if it's not in your offer letter. An executive's job is mostly mental so you need a physical release to balance your day-to-day activity. Cardio is by far the best exercise to maintain a good mental balance, then stretches or yoga and finally strength exercises. Golf, tennis and racquetball are good at integrating exercise and social but you need the cardio component big time. Insist on that gym membership.

Relocation Assistance

If you need to move your household to meet your new employment responsibilities, you should expect the company to offer a relocation package. This package should include travel costs for you and your family, moving costs for your household goods and other vehicles, hotel costs and some kind of per-diem. Some companies may also make provisions for the sale of your current house. If you are a hot prospect they may even offer to buy your house from you and immediately resell it.

Ask your employer what they will do. A good way to go about that is to draw up a realistic list of all relocation expenses. Give the list to your HR liaison and say, "If I have to incur these expenses, the company will cover it, right?"

They will then tell you what they will cover, specifically. Note: there is room for negotiation here, since every situation is different—even if they say, "Company policy provides a set amount for relocation expenses." Be prepared to plead your case, and be aware that your HR liaison is not the final authority on this.

Talking to Your New Boss About Your Offer Letter

If you find you need to talk to your new boss about your offer letter, wait until you have a list of all the items you want to discuss with him or her. They are busy people and needing to have multiple conversations on the various items of contention in your offer letter will not reflect well on you. Try to cover everything in one meeting and provide a hard copy for him or her to use as a check list. Follow this up immediately with an electronic copy so he or she can distribute it to other personnel to carry out the changes or get approvals.

Remember, this may be your first working encounter with your new boss—make it a good one. It will need to be clear, short (main points only) and organized with options. I have always found options to be extremely valuable in these affairs. Think it out for them. This helps you in two ways:

1. They don't have to strain their brain for what they see as non-work-related issues

2. You get to create the solutions, which will be naturally in your favor

Deliver your presentation professionally. This sounds simple but remember you may be dealing with items like health plan or relocation that affect not just you but your family. It will be easy to become emotional, especially if your premise is challenged. Believe me, it's not a typical business meeting. Character flaws will be noticed and remembered, so proceed cautiously. Composure and organization are your allies here.

Loans

Most companies offer this privilege to only senior executives. Moving loan programs are designed for an individual moving into an area, such as Silicon Valley, with more expensive real estate. Although the company may offer to buy your house from you, there may not be enough equity in your old home to allow you to buy a new one in a neighborhood befitting your new position. The company may consider extending you a home loan at a low interest rate to cover the difference. This is decided upon on an individual basis. So you must ask and be prepared to plead your case. This is not a small thing, clearly, and it will help you to understand how committed the company is to you. You will need to do your homework. Consult a knowledgeable realtor (an inexpensive way to get information) and have a real estate attorney review the agreement (worth paying for the important stuff).

Sign-on Bonus

If you have been told that you will receive a "signing bonus" or a "sign-on bonus" you should expect a clause like this in the offer letter:

You will receive a one-time sign-on bonus of $10,000.00 to be paid within thirty (30) days from your start date. Should you leave the Company within one year of your start date, you agree to repay the Company an amount pro-rated based on the number of months worked, at the time of termination.

A $20,000 sign-on bonus is not an outrageous number for an executive, but be careful. Your main play is for power: E-staff meetings, decision-making and direct access to senior management are the kinds of things that really matter over the long term. My experience has shown that most companies really respect their officers and a signing bonus is commensurate with industry and regional norms. If you have been an executive, or close to it, you already know what these numbers should be, unless you are moving to a new location. If that is the case, the information discussed in Chapter 4—Internet Job Hunting—should have helped you make a few friends in the new company who can provide you with data points to ferret out this kind of info.

Again, be alert to what you are agreeing to. If you are taking a risk with this employer or you think a better position is opening soon in another company that you see as a better fit, bank the signing bonus and don't spend it. I personally don't like this kind of approach because you can anger a lot of folks in your industry and burn bridges. Having said that, I understand that working to feed your family today may require different strategies and tactics. My parting thought is to be careful what you get known for in your industry.

"At Will Work"

In the "Term of Employment" section of the offer letter you may see "at-will" employment. Here's an example of what this clause looks like:

Term of Employment: Your employment with the Company is "at-will." In other words, either you or the Company can terminate your employment at any time for any reason, with or without Cause and with or without notice (subject to the provisions above concerning payment of severance benefits).

This kind of employment is usually offered by a fast-moving company with a start-up mentality: if you don't work out they don't want to spend a lot of time getting you out. They sell it to you by saying, if you want to move on you are free to do so. It's essentially employment for the commitment-shy, most often the employer. This is not necessarily a bad thing for everyone, just know what it means: your employment is tenuous.

With "Cause"

Again, this is a term or condition of employment. It's not something bad, unless you end up giving the company cause through misconduct or negligence. To protect yourself, however, you should know this is how you are being employed. If your offer letter contains a lot of legal language that you don't fully understand, bring it to an attorney with either corporate legal or employment law credentials.

"Cause" for termination will exist at any time after the happening of one or more of the following events: (i) employee's willful misconduct or gross negligence in performance of employee's duties hereunder, including employee's refusal to comply in any material respect with the legal directives of the Company's Board of Directors, President or Chief Executive Officer, so long as such directives are not inconsistent with employee's position and duties, and such refusal to comply is not remedied within ten (10) working days after the written notice from the Company, which written notice shall state that failure to remedy such conduct may result in termination for Cause; (ii) dishonest or fraudulent conduct, a deliberate attempt to do an injury to the Company, or conduct that materially discredits the Company or is materially detrimental to the reputation of the Company, including conviction of a felony; or (iii) employee's material breach of any element of the Company's Proprietary Information and Intellectual Property Agreement, including without limitation, employee's misappropriation of the Company's proprietary information.

This is a standard item in an offer letter. Read your offer carefully so you know what is expected of you and where the boundaries are. Again if the legal language is not completely clear, have an attorney review it. It's worth the money.

Severance Agreement

Coming on as an executive can be very delicate. Senior Management has an idea of what role you will play, and if you've asked the right questions during the interview process, you have a very clear picture of what that is. However, how you actually play that role is left to your discretion. A good senior management staff will give you latitude to express your own executive style. Yet until you are actually working in your new position it won't be obvious if your style is compatible with senior management's style of functioning. Usually a few one-on-one meetings early on help both sides adjust to each other. Sometimes, at this level, egos get involved and parties find themselves at loggerheads. As such, it's not uncommon for an executive to make provisions for a severance agreement in the offer letter. It's an insurance policy.

Your main concern with the severance package is that you have sufficient monetary resources to sustain you until you find another job. Executive positions take a while to secure, because the vetting process is thorough—after all, you come on board as an officer of the company, with a position of authority and power. The severance is designed to sustain you during this transition. In most cases 3-6 months of your base salary will satisfy that concern. Another issue to consider in a severance agreement is health care coverage. Make sure you have the option to continue in the health care plan for 6 months to a year.

Here's a sample clause to give you a better idea of what a Severance clause may look like in your offer letter:

Severance: In the event you are terminated by the Company (or any successor to the Company) without Cause (as defined in Appendix A), you will receive as severance the equivalent of four months' base pay   ($58,333.32), payable ratably over a period of six (6) months from the date of termination; provided that as a condition to such severance payment, you execute an agreement in form acceptable to the Company providing for a general release of any claims you may have against the Company, its officers, directors, stockholders and agents, and confirming the terms of your confidentiality and non-solicitation agreement with the Company.

While the sample above concerns itself with monetary compensation, you'll want to be sure that the complete Severance Agreement includes language addressing stock options and health care.

Note that this severance clause mentions an additional instrument, the "Release of Claims Agreement". This is SOP (Standard Operating Procedure). The company simply wants to be able to close the door once termination is complete. By the way, the release form is not ironclad. I have been a direct witness to instances where a terminated employee signed a release but felt wronged, hired an attorney and sued the company. In one such case the company knew it was a fake claim—a scam, essentially—but elected to settle for an amount equal to its insurance limit ($25,000) to avoid a public hearing. It was clear that the employee was running a kind of scam.

I'll say it once again—be careful what you get known for in your industry.

Summary

1. As an executive, power is more important than money—the compensation is usually there so spend your negotiation chips on the power elements

2. The power elements to focus on are:

   • being part of the decision-making process

   • participating in E-staff meetings

   • one-on-one meetings with senior management

3. When negotiating offer terms with your new boss, try to discuss all items of concern in one meeting: in your first working meeting make sure your points are well composed and professionally stated, and always provide options

4. Carefully read the legal rule of the hire; if it's not completely clear hire an employment attorney to help you

This material may not seem very exciting, but these are the nuts and bolts of your employment. These terms and conditions are really where the rubber meets the road for a job-hunter, and it's a must for you to know this information cold. You will be held accountable to your contract. Learn it, help re-structure it—and be prepared to honor it.

CHAPTER 10
CAREER TRACK MANAGEMENT

Beginning with this chapter the book takes on a new mission. Having given you the tools to pursue and capture a job, we'll look at growing your professional persona into the future.

The title of this book speaks to the psychic essence of the job hunt. Finding your inner predator is essential to going after a career. Knowing what kind of hunter you are helps you understand which way to take your career once you've started it. Seeing and developing your career personality traits is crucial to your long-term success. Take some time to study yourself: it's on the basis of owning your identity that true direction is found.

Throughout the book I've taken occasional side-bars, offering career track management advice. I'm going to collect all those gems into one place in this chapter so you can refer to it as a guide as junction points arise in your career.

My years of experience have given me a birds-eye view of career tracks, and where they usually lead over the long haul. By sharing this information, I hope to help you plan your direction. Sometimes these choices are a matter of looking deeply into your own nature, while at other times it's helpful to be exposed to new possibilities. Whatever it is that brings you to this crossroads take some time to not only think your new options through but also feel them from a quiet place inside.

Decisions are not always a product of intellectual deduction. Many times we encounter an invisible, persistent hint of where to go, one that won't be ignored. Ultimately, these are not even your choices to make. I know that many times these decisions will turn you inside out. However, I'm sure that at this point in your life you know all too well what I'm talking about. Let me see if I can provide a little light to make your journey clearer.

I'm not going to launch into a career seminar here by breaking down all possible careers and what's best for you. My purpose is to help you understand career tracks within your current field: individual contributor vs. manager, consultant vs. employee, resumé building and industry evangelist.

Individual Contributor vs. Manager

Very early in your career you need to know whether you are an *individual contributor* or a *manager*. Each has its own path, and you can't afford to lose time in your career development.

It's easy to get "typecast" early in your career. You may be bright and quite capable yet unwittingly find yourself building a career in the wrong track. If you start with a company in a technical position it's likely that your next promotion will be further in that direction. But is that really the best use of your talents? For some people, there's no doubt that it would be. Others may only discover after they've begun their career that they are cut out for a managerial role—or vice versa. Some time can go by before either you or your bosses recognize that.

Individual contributors love the technology or at least are very proficient in it. They are more interested in creating innovative breakthroughs in their field than in managing others. It's not uncommon for them to feel that managing actually slows them down.

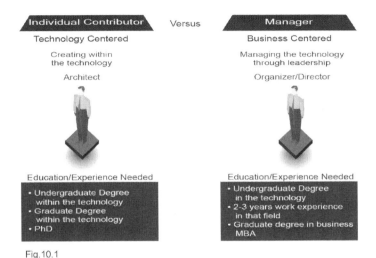

Fig. 10.1

Managers, on the other hand, are interested in the technology but prefer to manage it rather than create it. They seek to rise through the hierarchy as team leader, group manager, director, vice president and so on.

Determining which career track is most suited to your personality takes an honest assessment of your personality traits and of your abilities and potential skill level. If you are going to be part of the creative side of the company you had better know the technology inside and out. The individual contributor wakes up thinking about innovation, attempts to create a structure for it in the day and dreams about technological innovation at night. Is this you?

These people are usually systems architects. They comprise about 5% of the workforce. The next 20% of the work force understand, appreciate and work to implement the innovation. These are the managers, and the rest pretty much follow their direction. Managers, in my opinion, can be created, but architects are born. If you feel like you are the architect type, go for it. The worst that can happen is you'll end up with a marketable skills set translating the technology to senior management. Note that excellent managers earn more than technology architects, and have a broader range of options.

Though each track has its advantages, becoming a manager or an individual contributor is not so much a matter of choice as the result of an honest and accurate assessment of yourself. Talk it over with your friends, teachers, mentors—even your boss. You may be surprised at how helpful he can be.

So, what do you do to prepare your career?

The individual contributor needs to bury him or herself in the technology, earning not only an undergraduate degree in the field, but a graduate degree—including, ultimately, a PhD.

The manager type needs an undergrad degree in the technology along with some technical work experience, and then an MBA. Your resumé will say *I know my way around the technology, but I understand the business end of the industry, too*—prime stuff for a management path. A minimum of 2 years and a maximum of 6 years working with technology before moving on to your MBA is ideal.

Consultant vs. Employee

I took up this question in Chapter 2. Let's consider it a little more closely here.

Consultants fall into 3 general categories:

1. Entrepreneur – establishing a consulting firm

2. Employee – working for a consulting firm

3. Contractor – selling your skill set directly to clients

The entrepreneur may never actually do the consultant work. Their business model is to market the skill set of the technical specialists they represent. A consulting firm often grows organically—the principal may start as an actual consultant but then, as referrals and return business grows, the demand may outpace the individual's capacity. With a tweak here and there and good networking the principal can find himself making more money brokering a deal between a capable technical type and a client who needs help. A consulting firm is born.

The growth of the firm may be planned, as well. The founder may have seen a growing demand for designers or specialized engineers and is now actively striving to exploit this new market. I discussed developing a consulting firm in detail in Chapter 2 under "Consultant." If you are drawn to this kind of entrepreneurial approach I suggest you re-read it. I outline the three most fundamental principles behind launching a consulting venture and the driver for success.

An employee consultant actually works for a consulting firm. The firm hires you out to a client company, which assigns you to a given task. Sometimes employee consultants are actually contractors themselves, who are in turn subcontracted to the client.

As an employee contractor you may be able to contract yourself out to several consultant firms to ensure a steady flow of work. It can be a good way for a skilled specialist or engineer to ride out recessionary periods when corporations are slow to hire.

Some prefer this kind of work because it lets them focus on a particular type of project while maintaining an independence from duties generally associated with being employed. At the end of the project they can take a break, enjoying their freedom before accepting another assignment—when and where they want.

The last category of consultant is that of contractor. These specialists may simply want to work with a particular aspect of the technology. They are good at it and don't want to do anything else. Building their own consulting firm would take them away from the technology. This individual contributor type tends to have little interest in marketing or business management. They like to keep things simple.

If they are really good, work just comes to them. They schedule it as time permits. They aren't worried about losing clients; they have come to accept that they can't preserve their reputation by rushing through a project to get to the next one. The quality of their work is more important than the quantity. This is the reason they are in demand.

So what are the pros and cons of being a consultant versus being an employee?

A consultant practice is a business, be it small or large. There is freedom in being your own boss, like selecting the projects you work on, but once a project is done you must put on your marketer's hat and find more work if you don't have another one lined up. Some folks like this because it lets them step away from their specialty. However, others find they just don't have the personality for marketing. You need to be honest with yourself about this.

On the other hand, the employee does not get to select their next project but doesn't have to worry about hunting down his next project either.

The employee's taxes are a lot simpler, too. Taxes play a big role in managing your business, if you're a consultant. You get paid a lump sum for your work and are responsible for paying your own taxes. While you will have many more business tax deductions, an accounting system is a must to keep track of all this. In some cases, paying bookkeeper or accountant costs. The employee has less deductions, but taxes overall are far simpler because your employer simply takes them out of your pay.

There is a perennial debate about which is a better career choice—consultant or employee. For the most part it's a matter of personality. The two types of careers are very different, as are the lifestyles that come with them. Talk not only to your friends and mentors but to people who are consultants, they will be the most informative.

Resumé Building

Resumé building is really career management. A good way to approach your career is to build it horizontally and vertically. If you see yourself in a senior management role someday, then you should plan for that from the start.

Let's look at *vertical expansion* first. It really starts when you are taking upper division courses or technical courses in college. A technical degree is your goal. Own the fundamental principles of your field—the nuts and bolts. A solid foundation will let you take advantage of new advances in the technology as they come along—and they will, all the time.

Then get a job in your field. This is a must. If you aren't finding openings, become an intern. Your power is in the knowledge of your field. You need to learn more—and put it into practice—in a corporate setting.

Once you have gotten into the workplace, *check in* with yourself to decide whether you are an individual contributor or a manager at heart. In either case, work for 2-6 years, than go back to school. If you are an individual contributor, a specialist, get a higher degree in your field. If, on the other hand, you are a manager-to-be, get an MBA.

Your time in the industry will have shown you which companies are the key players. Do what you can to work your way into those top-tier companies. Then use the four-step process outlined in Chapter 12—Strategic Skills Development —to enhance your career. You are on your way.

Now let's discuss *horizontal expansion*. This axis of your career also begins in school but it's the development of your social network that we are interested in here. Make friends with talented and motivated people in your field of study. In college we tend to see the same people all the time. What you want to do here is extend yourself a little bit. Spend quality time with as many of them as time and circumstance permit. Have them talk about themselves. Get an idea of who they are, what their goals are, where they have been.

When you get to know people in this way, you will most often find that they are interesting and informative. Keep in touch with these folks after graduation. Over time, you will help them and they will help you. This exchange of ideas and contacts at the undergraduate level will not only forge strong, lifelong friendships, it will pay itself back in innumerable benefits over the course of your career.

Once in your first job, try to learn your position not just vertically, but horizontally as well. See if your boss will let you transfer into different groups to get a better understanding of the workflow, and what happens to it before it reaches your group— and after. This kind of shift will broaden your knowledge of the process. Lateral moves like that will prime you for overseeing projects, groups, departments and even small companies. In this way, you will be planning your way into senior management.

RESUMÉ BUILDING

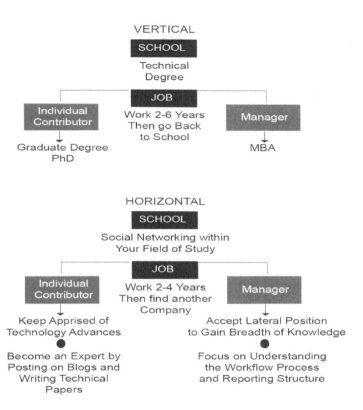

VERTICAL

SCHOOL

Technical
Degree

JOB

Individual
Contributor

Work 2-6 Years
Then go Back
to School

Manager

Graduate Degree
PhD

MBA

HORIZONTAL

SCHOOL

Social Networking within
Your Field of Study

JOB

Individual
Contributor

Work 2-4 Years
Then find another
Company

Manager

Keep Apprised of
Technology Advances

Accept Lateral Position
to Gain Breadth of Knowledge

Become an Expert by
Posting on Blogs and
Writing Technical
Papers

Focus on Understanding
the Workflow Process
and Reporting Structure

Fig.10.2

Be sure to work in each company between 2-4 years before looking for another company. You don't want to look like you can't hold a job. The fact that you are going to another company with a different title should help show your new company that the moves are strategic. If the job market is poor you may want to try some of those position transfers within the same company. Sooner or later you will have to change companies to show you can work your magic somewhere else, too.

This can get tricky during the interview if your hiring manager realizes what you are doing, and asks something like, "So, how long do you intend to stay with us?"

"Long enough to make us all look good," is not a bad answer, especially if you can say it with a laugh. But you should know that there will be hiring managers that recognize you are resumé building and won't hire you for that reason. They will assume you have a mercenary mentality, with no loyalty to anyone. There is nothing you can do about their perception.

Ideally you are doing this type of job hunting while you already have a job, with several target companies in mind. In other words, don't sweat it. It's more important to build your career than to please an overprotective, inflexible hiring manager. Keep your eyes on the prize, and keep climbing.

Short Term vs. Long Term Manager

In Chapter 8 I illustrated how a turnaround expert could be offered a department head position after turning that department back into a profit center. As tempting as that might seem, I mentioned, these are two different types of jobs that can be worlds apart.

Again, it all comes down to knowing what kind of person you are. Are you driven by creating order out of chaos? Do you prefer a fast-paced environment? Does slow and steady describe you better? Do you like wearing many hats? Do you want to build a work environment that can grow really large?

In the same chapter, I told a story about a sharp, "early stage guy" who liked starting with 3-5 key people, building the company to around 40 people then moving on and doing it again. He clearly knew his niche—you could say he was a master of that sweet spot. And that is why he was so successful.

Just as we asked you whether you saw yourself as an individual contributor or a manager, you need to know if you are "slow and steady" or "the rocket". Work tempo comfort is a variable often overlooked by many career professionals.

Just as before, if you are not sure, talk this point over with friends, teachers, mentors or your boss. It's important to nail this down so you can fine-tune your direction. Remember, seeing and developing your career personality traits is crucial to your long-term success. Take some time to study yourself.

Evangelizing

I love this concept. Near the end of Chapter 2 I proposed evangelizing as an option for the unemployed executive having trouble re-entering his own industry. The tactic doesn't need to be restricted to executives, however.

After reading Chapter 12 on Strategic Skills Development you will understand the four-step process to research and analyze your industry—understanding it like an expert. So why don't people treat you like an "expert," then? Two words here, predictions and publicity.

Predictions first. With a broad and informed knowledge of the industry comes the ability to create sound predictions. There are plenty of places to test those predictions before going public and attaching your name to them. Anonymous, industry-related chat rooms are a good place to start.

Once you feel good about your predictions, write them up in your industry blog, and send articles to both online and print trade journals. Be sure to keep all your work both published and unpublished. You are building a portfolio on a particular topic. You will add to this topic from time to time, and when you become known and respected, the entire portfolio can be launched as a series or converted into a training workshop. [Tip: Take screen shots of your work in online publications, because you ultimately have no control over their archiving process.]

If your industry has played a recognizable role in the economy (and really, what industry doesn't?), go ahead and submit your best articles to major business newspapers, including *The Wall Street Journal*.

The possible forms this kind of evangelism can take ranges from articles, blogs and white papers and books to webinars, and lectures, consulting engagements or on-site training. If you are an expert, an evangelist of your industry, you have many options, depending on whether you are more of an introvert or extrovert. There is plenty of money in either line. And in both cases you will be dynamically involved in your field—even shaping it's future.

Summary

1. Career track management decisions are not always a product of intellectual deduction

2. Individual contributors are driven by the technology while managers are more interested in directing the action—know which one you are

3. Consultants fall into three categories:

   • Entrepreneur – establishing a consulting firm

   • Employee – working for a consulting firm

   • Contractor – selling your skill set directly to clients

4. Resumé building is career management—build it both vertically and horizontally

5. Short-term vs. long-term managers are worlds apart—examine if you are "slow and steady" or a "rocket"

6. Evangelizing your technology or industry can satisfy and reward both the introvert or the extrovert, and help you to shape the future

This chapter is the pivotal point between the job hunt and constructing an enhanced "you."

Most job hunting books stop after you get the job. But getting the job is just a start. Ultimately, to get the most out of your career, you have to get more out of yourself. So we want to help you uncover the power within that will give you real empowerment.

Getting you the job is simply to create of the platform for launching a full expression of you, the future you, the "you" that may never have to worry about struggling to get a job, ever.

Tighten your seat belt.

CHAPTER 11
NEGOTIATION STRATEGY
AND TACTICS

Counterpoint is the technique of combining two or more melodic lines in such a way that they establish a harmonic relationship, while retaining their linear individuality. – American Heritage Dictionary

The principles contained in this chapter come from my own experience in countless negotiations. I even created a system called "CounterPoint Solutions." This chapter is the essence of my system. I would consider it the first objective step in building the future "you"—hard practical knowledge useful in any aspect of business. These principles combined with the four steps in the building of "Strategic Skills" in Chapter 12, will serve as the foundation for your future advancements. Study them well.

Negotiation Intro

This model comes from inter-company negotiation strategies and tactics conducted in a corporate environment. It may seem like overkill but the principles revealed here will prove themselves invaluable over the course of your professional career. With this in your toolbox to launch an effective negotiation, you will never enter a high level negotiation unprepared—be it on your own behalf for an offer letter, a capital acquisition or an intercompany platform.

Negotiation Scope

- Conflict Resolution

- Restructuring of Terms and Conditions

- Outline a Memorandum of Understanding

The areas listed in the Negotiation Scope are those in which these negotiation techniques may be used. In carrying out the duties of your title it will become obvious to you when to employ these tools. As such, this list may grow or simply become more defined.

Conflict Resolution is a tool to settle a dispute that is hindering or impeding the flow of business. These conflicts can be either internal or external, or between individuals or groups. Once such a conflict arises it should be addressed immediately. A mediator respected by both sides should be introduced, or an authority with the power to settle the dispute.

Restructuring of Terms and Conditions: The world of business is in constant flux. As such, a deal that was brokered only yesterday can quickly outlive its usefulness and become invalid. These market shifts can be devastating to a company if standing agreements and contracts are not brought up to date, especially in a sudden down market. When the economic crash of 2008 hit, organizations everywhere had to undergo huge restructures to accommodate the new rules of the game. These kinds of moves were vital if the international economy—and most western governments—were to survive.

Memorandum of Understanding: preceding most complex contracts there are MOU's. A Memorandum of Understanding serves as a worksheet or general template for the contract. It also loosely binds the negotiating parties into a pre-agreement, helping to establish earnest intent for an agreement.

These three instances are probably the most common places for the use of formal negotiations. Of course, the principles behind these negotiations can govern simpler matters like negotiating the terms of your employment offer letter—and I'll leave it to your own creativity to find application for them in other ways.

Negotiation Structure

For the sake of illustration let's assume that the contract or agreement we are exploring is external, between your company and another company. As such, the structure will have three basic elements:

- Business

- Legal

- Senior Management

The Business component is where the interface with the other side takes place. These exchanges address the business reasons for an agreement and sorts out how the agreement needs to look to deliver mutual benefit.

Legal crafts the language that captures the essence of the agreement while protecting the interests of the company.

Senior Management welcomes the other side and mutually celebrates the new partnership.

The Business Piece: All the negotiation is done in, what I like to call The Pit. This is where the representatives from each side sit down and hash out the key issues of concern for their respective sides. Since both representatives are professionals and very familiar with this process this business piece usually moves quickly. Neither negotiator has an ego investment in the matter and they are mainly concerned with reaching a point of mutual agreement. As such, The Pit is really more of a problem solving exercise than a battle of wills.

The Legal Piece: Once both representatives have reached what they feel is an agreement one of the parties will take their notes on the agreement to their own legal counsel to draft a contract. Given the choice I prefer to have my legal department work on that. Although the other side has counsel that will review and suggest changes in their favor there are always a few items that your own legal department put in the original document that will not be neutralized and that, of course, provides you with an advantage.

If you are one of the representatives in The Pit, be prepared to spell out each item you have agreed upon to Legal, and justify the need for it. It's Legal's job to protect the company and items that make good business sense in The Pit will not always make sense from Legal's point of view. You will be challenged, as well you should. The inclusion of Legal in the process is designed to provide support with checks and balances. It's your insurance policy against negotiation mistakes or oversights. Legal is not a hindrance but a protection.

The natural progression here calls for the completed contract (first draft) to be presented to the other side. Their counsel will review the contract and usually adjust it. Of course, your counsel will review and suggest changes to counter. This continues until all parties are satisfied. Once that happens the final draft is completed and the contract is signed.

Senior Management: Once the contract is signed the highest-ranking members of senior management present on both sides symbolically reaches across the table and shakes hands. This brings a nice, civil conclusion to the process.

Senior management usually watches this process from afar, staying out of the negotiation. However, at the conclusion of the negotiation, it's fitting for the CEO or President of the company to welcome and congratulate the other side in a celebration that highlights the upside of the agreement.

Negotiation Philosophy

Be aware of both the tangible and intangible collateral components contained within any given agreement. Although at some point it may be necessary to reveal the iron fist within the velvet glove, we always strive to end the agreement with a meaningful handshake.

No matter how big the industry, the landscape of corporate players becomes very small when it comes to inter-company deals. You will certainly encounter your counterpart in this negotiation again, directly or indirectly. In the interest of preserving of long-term relationships, it behooves you to conclude an agreement professionally. Never forget this.

Negotiation Process

The following are the nuts and bolts of what goes on in the Pit. This is the core of the process—the distillation of many years of negotiations:

1. Preliminary meeting with your counterpart to discuss the current agreement generally, for the purpose of understanding:

    • Why there will be an agreement

    • What value this agreement has for their side

    • Why are they even willing to discuss a positive outcome

Extract as many positive reasons from your counterpart as you can, to emphasize the value of this agreement. These positive reasons can play an important role in subsequent, difficult negotiations, reminding the two sides why they are here.

2. Probe deeply into any obstacles your counterpart sees that are preventing both sides from moving forward now.

3. Evaluate these obstacles carefully—they may list several points of objection but when pressed you are likely to find only one or two of them are really deal-breakers.

4. Once you have encountered any deal-breakers, push your counterpart to find their level of minimum satisfaction. That is, what is the least it would take to get them to move forward or compromise on those issues. Having found that out, break off talks to re-group with our own stakeholders.

5. Meet with stakeholders on your side and detail an offer. The strategy for the offer will be of two types.

- Determine the highest value you are willing to offer for this agreement, offer it and hold firm.

- Determine the highest value you will pay, but offer a lesser amount—an amount that borders on being insulting. In this case you are prepared for a counter offer. This also allows the opportunity for you to extend face-saving concessions to the other side later, as needed.

Deciding which method to use is based subjectively on your personality type. But the strategy for framing the offer is extremely important and will require careful deliberation. The way you frame the offer is as important as the offer itself.

6. Present your written offer with a deadline date for signature reply.

7. Either collect the signed agreement or prepare for another round of negotiation (Step 2).

It is necessary to know when to push, how hard to push, and even when to escalate the negotiations to the breaking point. It is also necessary to know when to back off, concede, and even genuinely befriend your counterpart. This kind of give and take will happen many times throughout the negotiations. The art is in knowing when to use what, and how much is enough. These intangibles are the value proposition. This is what experience teaches.

You will conduct many negotiations within the span of your professional career. With each one you will further develop these skills. I always enjoyed difficult negotiations because the most challenging encounters pushed my limits and in the end, made me better at what I do.

Summary

1. Development of negotiation skills are a must for advancement in business

2. The most common negotiation applications are:

    - Conflict Resolution – either internal or external

    - Restructure of Terms and Conditions – to suit current market conditions

    - Outline an MOU – as a precursor to drafting a binding contract

3. The three elements of the negotiation structure are:

    - Business – The Pit – where negotiation takes place motivated by business sense

    - Legal – designed to provide support with checks and balances to protect the company's interest

    - Senior Management – not directly involved in negotiations until the handshake that concludes the deal, welcoming and celebrating the newly established partnership or agreement

4. Negotiation Philosophy – respect the tangible and intangible components and strive to end the agreement with a meaningful handshake

5. Negotiation Process

- Draw from your counterpart the strongest reason they have for entering negotiations

- Find out what your counterpart sees as the greatest obstacle to a successful outcome

- Assign values to the other side's demands – locate the deal-breakers

- Probe your counterpart on what will minimally satisfy those deal breakers

- Meet with your own stakeholders to craft an offer and a strategic delivery of that offer

- Present your written offer, properly framed, with a deadline date for signature

- Either collect the signed agreement or prepare for another round of negotiation

This chapter may seem basic in nature but it comprises a powerful addition to your tool box. This is designed for the building of an individual who has an eye on the future. If you play the game for the sake of survival, you won't—advancement is the name of the game. It is only by going for it, and aiming for the top rung, that you not only survive but excel.

Your goal is to build an invincible "you." This isn't motivational chatter. It's a real assertion.

CHAPTER 12
STRATEGIC SKILLS DEVELOPMENT

The key component in going from management to senior management (two levels from manager to director to VP) is the development of strategic skills. Many large corporations target managers for management development programs. The idea is to grow skilled senior managers, who know their firm's system, from their own ranks. Why look for managers used to another system if you can turn your own top producers into real aces?

In selecting management prospects, the single most sought-after skill set is "strategic thinking." The business world is clearly a goal-oriented environment. Successful goals come from solid plans, and planning has its roots in strategy. So we can say that strategic planning is the basis for all successful business. It's no wonder that all companies have an eye out for the strategic-minded managers.

If you want to be in the highest tier of management you have to have vision. Strategic thinking is not simply an inborn personality trait, however. Or a skill that only comes from many years of business experience. It can be a learned skill set. I have thought about this for some time and have developed a four-step process to develop strategic thinking.

If you have the slightest interest in knowing how your industry works there is no reason why you can't build on that natural curiosity to develop strong strategic thinking habits. You selected the industry you did because you were attracted to it and with that attraction comes a curiosity for knowing what makes it tick. That healthy curiosity is all you need to nurture your strategic thinking.

Cultivate that curiosity through this four-step process, implement the key components and you will be transformed. Your higher-ups will see you differently, your industry I.Q. will rise and you will become a serious contributor. You will never feel at a loss in your field of work. Read these four steps once through to get a feel for them. Roll up your sleeves, read it again to personalize and schedule the action points it contains.

This could be the single most important secret weapon you have for your own career advancement. So take the bull by the horns.

Research

Find business information sites (with current data) relevant to your particular niche industry. If your niche industry is too small to get significant useable data step it up to the larger industry. Review them regularly. You can do this on weekends or after work but establishing a schedule for this ensures that it gets done. If you are serious about advancing in your field then checking on the well-being of your industry and niche industry should be of natural interest to you.

Sign up for news alerts about your industry and target companies, which can be done for free on many sites. Hard copy trade journals are well worth the cost, as well. Study your industry both from within and without—that is, know what others are saying about your industry. There is nothing like third-party perspectives to broaden your vision.

Find chat rooms that are discussing your niche industry. See if you can join relevant discussion groups on LinkedIn. Focus on specific topics. Make charts, schematics and diagrams of the economic and technological drivers in your industry. With new technology emerging ever faster, you must know what it is and how thought leaders in your space think it will shape the industry. Understand how your industry really functions. Who are the players, the innovators, the naysayers? Learn about its history, its predicted future.

I spent several years as VP and co-founder of a wind farm land acquisition company. I subscribed to wind farm, renewable energy, fossil energy, utilities, government energy and environmental journals to name a few. I'd read articles put out by farmer's publications, wind tower construction firms, wind turbine manufacturers to keep up with my industry, and I'd bookmark articles on renewable energy trends in Canada, Europe, South America and Asia. I'm the first to admit I'm not an avid reader, but I knew I needed to know my industry from every angle. Knowledge is power.

Analysis

As you collect industry data, comb it for short, medium and long-term patterns. Make notes, review them regularly, and test if a pattern you think you've found holds up over time.

Reading information on industry performance is one thing but analyzing that data is something else. If you are a spreadsheet person create charts to track your findings. If you are not that kind of person, then keep a running journal on what events occurred and when. Write your opinion on what you think caused a particular event based on what you know from the array of data points you have been monitoring.

Write your opinion in a distinctive color and be sure to date your entries. This will help if you detect a trend later on and want to back-track events that may not have been obvious at the time of your notations. This will be valuable to help you restructure causal events that may have been responsible for a trend or market shift. In this way, you can discover patterns and sequences that signal early stages of trends—predictors, if you will. If you find you can accurately predict a market trend based on your analysis of previous events, you will be ready to make a powerful addition to a work group—or a new company.

When you read something later about an event that describes why it occurred, enter that in your notes or journal with yet a different color. This will allow you to see how well your own analysis matches with that of the "experts." Note: as you get better at this, and more knowledgeable about the subject, you may mentally challenge the opinion of the experts. When that happens and you feel ready to engage in a detailed argument against those experts, you know you are ready for prime time.

Creation

Write strategies based on your findings that benefit your immediate group/company/industry.

As your opinions become developed enough to stand on their own, write them down. This writing can be done in bullet format at first, just to capture the essence, but get them down on paper, or in a file on your laptop or phone. You are building something here…later, you will need to know how you got there. If your idea is fleshed out enough to write an article, blog or paper, label it well so the title of the document will remind you of what's in it at a later date.

Testing

When you feel you are ready, air your analysis in your group meeting see if it holds up to the group's scrutiny.

Select an opinion that you see as appropriate for the group. It should be solid, both in that it's well-researched and likely to stand up to inquiry (in your estimation) when viewed by people in your group. You may even want to test your theory on a friend in the industry first to see if he or she can poke holes in it. Eventually, though, you just have to throw it out there.

Many things can happen during this exercise. Your analysis may be received without much comment and seemingly forgotten. That's OK. You can continue to work up your second opinion and prepare it for launch at another meeting. After a while someone will notice and comment on it.

Your opinion piece may be challenged, with lots of holes poked in it. This is good. You now know who you need to satisfy and what their basic philosophy is. This is valuable feedback. Can you make your opinion better? Of course you can. Go back to work on it. You are now really motivated. There is nothing like a challenge to inspire someone.

In this process it won't take long before a manager takes note of your pro-active engagement, your intellectual curiosity and your desire to be a bigger contributor. Remember, you are in a merit-based environment. Even if you have just presented a controversial analysis, you are quickly increasing your value. Even if your company is a dog and doesn't want to give you a promotion or a raise, you are still ahead of the game.

By this time you will really know the industry, its trends, the top tier players and the future direction of the industry. You have equipped yourself with knowledge. Ideally, your current company sees that. If they don't, you are free to target your next employer. And you can do this while you are still working —that always makes you more attractive to prospective employers—so you won't skip a beat. It's your current firm's responsibility to see rising stars. They have first crack at you. If for whatever reason they show little or no interest, you must act. Make all your hard work pay for itself. Take control of your destiny. This is real empowerment.

Strategic Skills Development

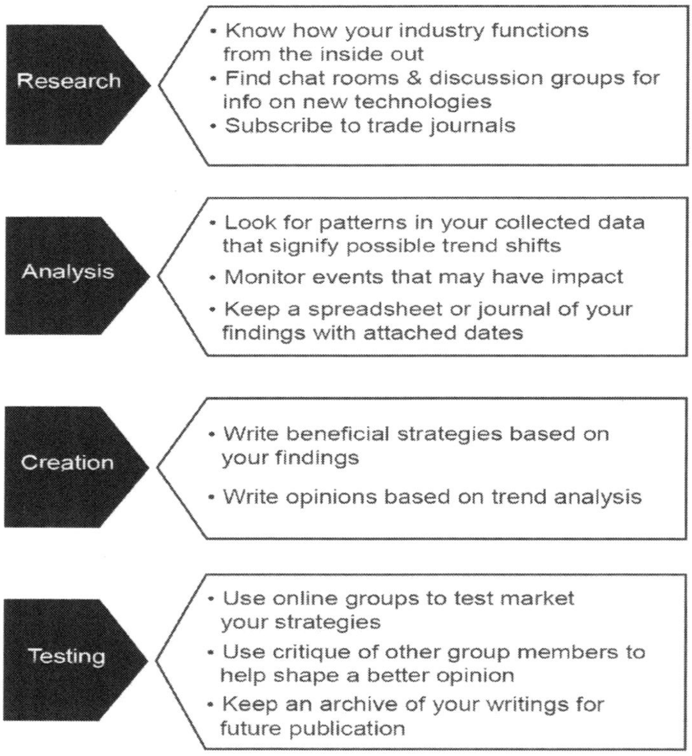

Research
- Know how your industry functions from the inside out
- Find chat rooms & discussion groups for info on new technologies
- Subscribe to trade journals

Analysis
- Look for patterns in your collected data that signify possible trend shifts
- Monitor events that may have impact
- Keep a spreadsheet or journal of your findings with attached dates

Creation
- Write beneficial strategies based on your findings
- Write opinions based on trend analysis

Testing
- Use online groups to test market your strategies
- Use critique of other group members to help shape a better opinion
- Keep an archive of your writings for future publication

Fig.12.1

Summary

1. The single most important skill set for job advancement as a manager is "strategic thinking"

2. Strategic thinking can be learned through this four-step process of Research, Analysis, Creation and Testing

3. Research is the study of your industry from within it and outside of it

4. Analysis is finding patterns and trends from your research that allows you to make your own predictions about your industry, independent of what "experts" have to say

5. Creation is the composition of a written industry premise that can be presented to your group or department

6. Testing is the presentation of your industry theory and the fielding of questions and comments

This entire process is designed to elevate your status and value within your group, company and niche industry, making you an empowered asset not only for your company but for your industry. This level of contribution will differentiate you and transform you into a leader with "Vision."

CHAPTER 13
AWARENESS

Awareness or consciousness is an abstract concept that appears to have no place in the concrete, practical world of business. The reality, however, is that awareness—inner and outer awareness—may be the most vital asset of the predator and the single most important success factor in any endeavor.

What do we mean by awareness? Awareness is the act of being alert, wakeful, focused. To be aware is to come into a situation with eyes open, cognizant of everything. When the mind is alert, an individual is tuned into the environment around them.

Usually, when we speak of awareness, we are referring to *outer awareness*. We are familiar with the channels of outer awareness—listening, seeing and sensing—extensions of the mind, through which information in the environment is gathered for evaluation, processing and action. We touched on this component of awareness early in this book when we talked about understanding and uncovering information, presenting ourselves in the most appropriate way, and formulating intelligent questions to increase our chances of getting the job.

The concept was, simply stated, "Outer awareness provides the questions."

It is through this question-and-answer dynamic—assisted by awareness—that the job hunter creates a relationship with the hiring manager, one that may lead to getting the job. The basic principle here is easy to understand: we have been using interactive dialog to establish relationships throughout our lives.

What is not so obvious is the concept of *inner awareness.* How does inner awareness help us answer questions and handle ourselves in an interview? More generally, how can it develop us in the direction of empowerment? Let's go into this phenomenon.

When someone asks us a question we take a moment, however brief, to think of the correct answer. Perhaps we think about why the question was asked. Maybe we know the answer, but we want to gauge how much to disclose. Sometimes we want to decide how to frame the answer for maximum impact. So for the most part we think before we answer.

Early in this book I encouraged you to "fall back on yourself" before answering questions in the hiring process. Particularly the difficult questions, pause and check in with you. That ensures that you won't give a hasty response you may regret. You give yourself more time to run through all your options—one of which might include asking a clarifying question to better understand the initial question. You can understand how this momentary pause can help you present yourself at your best in a critical discussion with a hiring manager and give yourself a better chance of getting the job.

But what about this idea of empowerment?

Falling back on the self, for most of us, simply means taking our awareness inward to the field of thinking. But can we go deeper?

Deeper than thinking is feeling. If we really want something our mind will work to determine how to get that thing. Those desires are deeper, more primary than our thinking—and more powerful—since they direct the mind to plan an action to fulfill that need or desire.

Can we go deeper still?

Those desires must have come from somewhere. As we have just deduced, that sense of wanting something is not only deeper than thought but it's more fundamentally powerful since it actually directs thought. Could there be a place that is both deeper and more powerful than the level of feeling?

This may seem like a more mystical dimension of inquiry. I would venture to say, that anyone who has ever meditated has attempted to find such a place, touched on it, or has actually found that place where those desires first emerge. It isn't beyond human comprehension.

How many times have you felt, just before waking up, that you weren't really sleeping but were not actually awake either? Perhaps there was a moment when everything around you was settled and you "spaced out," not on a thought or a feeling, but on basically...nothing. Maybe you were thinking about something, the thought had concluded, but you hadn't yet picked up the next thought—and for a short moment you were in a gap, a place of no thoughts. I could go on and on describing these quiet, perhaps fleeting moments where virtually nothing was happening. It's a state of stillness and of quiet. It's pleasant and unusually restful.

Once we've experienced it we want to have it again. But how?

We can have this state when we're awake and active. Very active, in fact—many people call it being in the "zone". The "runners high" comes to mind—top athletes have described these moments of great peace and clarity in the middle of intense and dynamic activity, even in an NFL playoff game. They usually talk about it as a quiet state where awareness was still and collected inside, even while the body was going through extreme activity.

It's a meditative state of awareness, yet you don't lose awareness of the world around you.

People meditate for the sake of experiencing that state. Afterwards, most everyone reports coming out with a sense of balance, peace and joyfulness. This is inner awareness—the awareness that can, if experienced on a regular basis, change the way you think, perceive and act. It's not too dramatic to say that it can change your life. I know because I've been practicing Transcendental Meditation for over 30 years.

Anyone who knows me will tell you that I am a very practical person. There is no way that I would continue a practice without seeing benefits on a regular basis. So, to continue something daily for over 30 years is really saying something.

You have come so far in this book learning how to take control, not by sheer force of will but by achieving a balance between sensitivity and intelligence. You have achieved a question and answer technique designed to manage, comfort and respectfully control your hiring manager. Perhaps without even realizing it, you have become more than you expected you could be. And you are not finished.

The most powerful tool for continued personal growth is awareness. Pick it up, push it to the limit. Work to become the best possible professional and the best possible person. As I mentioned in Chapter 1, our purpose is not to make you appear better by having you slap on fake attributes. We want to know that the readers of this book are discovering more fundamental, empowering values within themselves—and, are incorporating them, in a step by step fashion, into their behavior, becoming empowered from within.

Use this knowledge to shoot for the stars.

Summary

1. Awareness is the act of being alert, wakeful or focused

2. Awareness can be either of an outer nature or an inner nature

3. "Outer awareness provides the questions. Inner awareness provides the answers"

4. Through a question-and-answer dynamic you create a relationship with the hiring manager

5. Inner awareness provides two things: it guides us to answer questions and it develops empowerment

6. We can use inner awareness by falling back onto our thinking for a moment before answering

7. As we continue in the direction of inner awareness we discover that our feelings and desires come from a deeper place than our thinking

8. Falling back deeper we realize that beyond our feelings resides a field of stillness

9. Meditation gives those who practice it regularly the experience of stillness and a sense of inner quiet and happiness

10. A regular program of meditation can be good for anyone to help them develop not only peace and clarity but personal empowerment

We have explored a relatively abstract concept of awareness in a manner that allowed us to listen, see and sense others in the hiring process—observations that have been the basis for our questions. When the role is reversed and we are answering questions, a sense of inner awareness is very useful as well.

We have pushed beyond using inner awareness as a tool to answering questions during the hiring process to using it as a tool for self-development. This "inner research" can be pleasant and joyful, as well as empowering—enhancing our entire psychology and spirit. This more profound understanding of this simple tool of awareness may leave us with the thought, "How enhanced can I be?" I'd like to explore this in greater depth at the conclusion of the book.

SUMMARY

The first objective of this book was to approach the job hunt without being submissive—particularly in the interview. I began with the story of an experienced executive who exuded confidence and poise in his interview. His objective was clear —and in a very cordial manner he took control of the interview. While the candidate had years to perfect his persona, the way he handled himself gave us an example of the kind of job hunter we are striving to become: a predator, alert, hungry, absolutely focused on our goal.

For those readers who are in the early stages of developing themselves as a job hunter, I have used all my knowledge and experience to distill the techniques of these interview masters into a step-by-step approach to help you gain the kind of skill, control and awareness modeled by this executive.

It's a big and substantive goal, and we know you can't achieve it by trying on attributes you don't really feel inside. Instead, we've used the tool of awareness to direct your attention inward, locating and actualizing these qualities within yourself. These characteristics of mastery are ones we want to have in the job hunt, in our career, and in life. By showing you how to launch and conduct your professional life in the right way, we are bringing an element of empowerment to your career that can pay dividends well beyond the office.

As you may recall, the very first technique we uncovered in Chapter 1 was the art of balance to create respectful control. Control is a crucial element of "winning" the interview. Yet it's unlikely that my readers have the ability to turn the interview in the same way, that my executive job candidate displayed. I illustrated how an element of finesse could deliver the control component. I showed how the technique of respectful control lets you respond to the employer's agenda without compromising your own goals. That in itself is a victory. This is the intelligence of the predator at work.

In Chapter 2 we categorized the workforce into five sectors based primarily on the work skills they have achieved. For each of the five categories I provided options—again from a skills perspective—that offered a platform and a path for success. We learned that not having a strong, marketable skill set places us at a distinct disadvantage in the marketplace. By upgrading our skills, however, or perhaps just fine-tuning what we do have, we can positively affect our own outcome.

If Chapter 2 marked the beginning of skills development, then Chapter 3 moved us along to organizing and presenting those skills. First, we broke down skills into hard and soft skills. Hard skills are measurable and objectively verified: technical qualifications, years of experience, education, completion of deliverables or quotas met. Soft skills, on the other hand, are general and subjective in nature: character, passion for work, communication, problem solving, team awareness, initiative or work ethics.

From a presentation perspective, we confined hard skills to the resumé and put soft skills in the cover letter. We outlined a solid format for presenting these skills so that they formed a one-two punch to get us to the interview.

Chapter 4 looked at digital assets and how to leverage them in the job hunting process. We learned how to find the hidden job market; which job boards are right for you; how to use social and professional networks to find jobs and gather information about target companies; how to befriend employees in those target companies; and how to grow networks to benefit us over the course of our career. All this from your computer, tablet or smart phone.

In Chapter 5 the predator was born. Until this point we had been setting the stage; here we became pro-active and got serious about the job hunt. We targeted industry, niche industry, company and ultimately our new boss. Headhunter secrets were revealed for the first time. Including techniques that helped us track down our new boss. This was the time to make contact with him, even forming a partnership to assist us in getting a job. Here we experienced job hunting at its finest.

Chapter 5, the heart of the book, led to the brains of the book, Chapter 6, "The Interview." We went into interview psychology to completely understand the dynamics of the meeting between you and the hiring manager. Point by point, we broke down how to approach, appear and conduct yourself in an interview. From having your company research at hand, to what to except in the interview flow. Your demeanor in gaining control of the interview. How best to use your "questions list." Creating a colleague-to-colleague relationship with the hiring manager for the purpose of an in-depth discussion on workflow. We also showed you ways to set up your second interview—possibly even immediately—while still in your first interview. We touched on concluding the interview with a vision of a new plan for the work group in a way that ties you into a larger dynamic. This chapter alone, I feel, is worth the cost of the book because of the hard-won information it gives the job hunter. Through the skillful interaction of your newly actualized talents, you stepped onto the threshold of the predator in Chapter 5. With a little practice you will own this skill set in Chapter 6.

Chapter 7 tied up some loose ends, such as how to vet the interviewer and identify what his or her view is of your new position (you must always know who you are talking to). Then working to build the same interview psychology as you did with the hiring manager. In this chapter we also discussed the phone screen. Again, start by knowing who you are talking to —and where they are in the hiring process. Finally, we ended the chapter with information about the background check. The most telling moment in all this was the power that the prospective employer has in the world of social and professional networks to find out personal info about your private life. As we mentioned, there are services out there that can help you see what a background check may uncover and allow you to post a comment to help you defend or offer a disclaimer for the data.

Chapter 8 and 9 centered on providing you specific knowledge of the terms and conditions of an offer letter. You also learned how to make changes, through your new boss, to items you feel need improvement. In Chapter 9 we looked at the executive version of the offer letter, and learned how to acquire power by plugging into the decision-making process and the E-staff meetings.

In Chapter 10 the book took on a new mission. We started to move toward growing a professional persona for the rest of your career. We started by helping you determine which direction was the right one to take. This book is designed to build the job hunter from the inside out. So here we help you take an introspective look at your own career identity. Only by owning that identity can you find your true direction.

This chapter also brought back the concept of empowerment, in terms of developing both your career identity and your personal identity. As our career identity develops we will naturally find ourselves taking more control over our self-expression and then, increasingly, our general persona. While ownership of our career identity yields a stronger "you," we move through other aspects of our lives with more determination and purposefulness. This is how empowerment is being built from within.

Chapter 11 delivered a tool for the enhancement of the predator, with advanced tools. Our look at "Negotiation Strategy and Tactics" provides the first of these advanced tools—Chapter 12 delivered the next.

Negotiation know-how is intrinsic to effective business development. We took you from negotiation introduction through the seven steps of the negotiation process—a mini-course in itself. At the end you had all the crucial elements you need to winning negotiations.

If you were to learn only one objective component to advancement of your career it would be contained in Chapter 12, "Strategic Skills Development". "Strategic Skills" is the single most important element for career advancement in business today. We took you through a four-step process of research, analysis, creation and testing. You have the most powerful tool in business in your arsenal. Now, it's just a matter of activating it.

Up to now we have shown you job hunting psychology, headhunter's tactics, creative interview techniques, negotiation procedures and strategic skills development. In Chapter 13 we went deeply into the powerful subjective tool of awareness. We clearly revealed how outer awareness provides the questions (touching back to Chapter 6), while our inner awareness provides the answers. We also ventured a step closer to experiencing how inner awareness can deliver personal empowerment.

Conclusion

So where have we delivered you?

We have provided the objective knowledge you need to overcome submissiveness in the hiring process. We have showed you how to establish and maintain control at each step in the process. Not control through force of will, but respectful control through the balance of sensitivity and intelligence.

This element of balance has helped us weave our way through someone else's agenda without compromising our goals. This is the basis of the colleague-to-colleague relationship that is so essential to form with the hiring manager in your job interview. On the basis of this relationship we have tilted the interview in our favor, and opened the door to move the interview to a side-by-side session with the hiring manager where you can analyze and share new ideas for your new group. The entire interview dynamic should have portrayed you as a worthy addition to their team, providing a significant value-added proposition.

Once the offer letter is extended, you have detailed information on all the significant items in it—as well as how to adjust those items to upgrade the offer.

After becoming a new hire you have been given a full understanding of negotiation and strategic skills development that you need to comprehensively and quickly move ahead in your job and your career.

Sprinkled throughout this discourse has been an undercurrent of developing subjective skill sets—elements such as awareness, balance, respectful control and grace.

Both objective and subjective development, fused in a goal-oriented environment, have given you what you need to get the job. Our broader mandate in putting together this mosaic was to build the job hunter of the future.

This blueprint has now been delivered in its entirety. The torch has been passed. The responsibility now rests on your shoulders to transform this knowledge into action, and the action into achievement, and the achievement into fulfillment.

You must now find your way to win.

ABOUT THE AUTHOR

Energy entrepreneur, Silicon Valley headhunter, counselor for at-risk youth and combat helicopter pilot, Jim Rocca has been finding a way to win his whole life. His first book, *Job Hunt Like A Predator,* taps Jim's business and recruiting experience to help readers turn the challenges of the job market into long-term career success.

Jim was a highly paid headhunter and corporate recruiter in Silicon Valley recruiting executives, software developers, professional services experts, marketing and public relations managers, among others. Jim worked with every department head throughout the organization, gaining an intimate familiarity with the internal operations of multinational, enterprise-class corporations.

He went on to co-found a land acquisition company servicing the world's three top wind farm developers, where he served as Vice-President.

Jim rejoined the business world after taking a 3 year time-out to counsel at-risk high school students in career selection and the development of marketable skills. To help his students, Jim developed a career assessment evaluator and a comprehensive career matrix with an approach of *pulling* rather than pushing the student to the goal. This tool helped foster a self-motivational dynamic that proved effective in launching students into successful careers.

As a U.S. Army helicopter pilot, Jim logged more than 1000 hours flying combat missions in Vietnam. Prior to receiving his B.A. at Maharishi University of Management in Iowa, Jim was part of a relay track team that set a national junior-college record, and started a successful moving and storage business with $140 to his name.

Jim is currently launching a series of hiring and career skills workshops based on *Job Hunt Like A Predator,* which he will deliver at colleges and universities around the country. *Job Hunt Like A Predator* is the first volume in Jim's three-part *Empowerment* Series, designed to develop men and women to their full, professional and personal potential.

Jim lives in Fairfield, Iowa with his graphic artist wife, Trish.

Empowerment Course

Our mission is to deliver the most effective technologies for successful job hunting, career planning and job advancement currently available.

Below you'll see, in bullet format, an overview of our course followed by a more detailed outline of the course. The subject matter can be tailored to suit your group's needs. The detailed outline is more like a menu of choices offered. Before we present the course to your group we expect to have at least one preliminary meeting with you, our client, to accurately determine what is most helpful for your group to get out of this course. We then restructure the course to reflect this in-put and send it back to the client for review and/or alteration.

Short Overview of the Course

Job Hunting

- Preparing the Hunter – skills development, organization and presentation

- The Internet as a Job Hunting Tool

- Aggressive Job Hunting through a pro-active system

- Shaping Interview Psychology to give the Job Hunter a competitive advantage

- Understanding the key components of the job offer to help you create better terms

- Teaching the success principles of Negotiation and Strategic Skills to advance one's career

Career Exploration

- All careers can be found in 12 career streams

- Comprehensive understanding of Certificate Programs as a career tool

- Where to search to find a deeper understanding of your career and related options

- The principle of "Follow your Passion"

Empowerment

- Tying together objective and subjective success principles to grow empowerment

- Fostering conditions for a psychological transformation to create an enhanced individual

- Building the persona of the future

Detailed Outline of the Course

Job Hunting

- ○ Preparing The Hunter
    - ○ Skills assessment and development for:
        - ▪ Little or non-skilled labor
        - ▪ College graduates without specific skills
        - ▪ Mature job candidates with general skills
        - ▪ Skilled labor
        - ▪ Executives

- Skills organization using Hard and Soft skills as a foundation

- Skills presentation through the Resumé and Cover Letter

- <u>The Internet as a Job Hunting Tool</u>

  - Techniques for finding the Hidden Job Market

  - How to befriend employees at your target companies

    - Getting valuable info about company culture, policies, hiring process, interview methods, benefits, etc

  - Job Boards – Monster, Hot Jobs, Dice, etc

  - Maximizing use of the King of on-line professional networks – LinkedIn

  - Self-Branding as a marketing tool

  - Search Engine Optimization (SEO) techniques so prospective employers can find you

- <u>Pro-Active Job Hunting</u>

  - How to dissect your target industry, niche industry and company

    - Using on-line services, financials, press releases, trade journals, etc

    - How many companies to target and how to spreadsheet the data for easy comparisons

- Using proven headhunter's secrets for finding and contacting your new boss

- How to get prospective hiring managers to help you in the job hunt

- <u>The Interview</u>

  - Modeled on the collection of a composite of successful executive interviews altered for everyone's usage

  - How best to prepare regarding company research, questions and reference materials

  - Interviewing Psychology – control, respect and grace
    - Communication on equal footing – not being submissive
    - Your business demeanor
    - Attire

  - Interview Flow – Your turn, their turn, your turn - transitions

  - Different Interview Methods – Traditional, Behavioral, Stress, Case, etc

  - Your interview questions and your objectives
    - Colleague relationship
    - Identifying the job responsibilities
    - Outlining the job in a schematic

- Introducing the opportunity for change
- Tying yourself to that change
  - Leveraging the Second Interview while still in the First Interview

Beyond Job Hunting

- The Job Offer – understanding it and negotiation of job title, compensation, signing and performance bonus, stock options, health and retirement benefits, etc

- Mini Courses for the advancement of one's Business Career

  - Negotiation Course
    - Negotiation, scope, structure, philosophy and seven step process

  - Strategic Skills Development
    - Four step process – research, analysis, creation and testing

Career Exploration

- All careers can be found in 12 career streams

  - Taking the career concept of People, Data and Things to the next level

  - Expanding the career matrix laterally in 4 stages from abstract to concrete

- Certificate Programs – their benefits and how to find the right one

  - Value-added proposition and career entry level component

  - Opportunity to be shaped by your field of interest

  - Free job placement service

  - Paid well

- Finding out more about your career and related optional careers

  - Prospects for the future, work environment, typical duties, education needed, national pay scale, similar careers, etc

- The principle of "Follow Your Passion" – Day Job vs. Night Job

Empowerment

- Tying together objective and subjective success principles to grow empowerment

  - Summarize the objective and subjective success principles illustrated in the course

  - Show how we built confidence, fine-tuned attitudes and utilized awareness

  - Outer awareness formulates the questions while inner awareness provides the answers

- ○ Fostering conditions for a psychological transformation to create an enhanced individual

    - ○ Understanding, "Live the dignity of your future potential, today" as a support system

- ○ Building the persona of the future

As mentioned earlier, please use the detailed course outline as a menu of possibilities that can be shaped to compliment your group's goals. We are available to help co-design a course that will serve as a tool for development of your individual and group objectives.

Most Sincerely,

Jim Rocca

jim_rocca@yahoo.com

INDEX

Job descriptions
clarification of, 71, 74–75, 91
confirm, at highest level of offer, 108, 118
posted, *vs.* outlining new positions, 77, 92
second interview and, 97, 103

Job hunting
evangelizing as part of, 28, 141*f,* 143–144, 145
goals and objectives in, 74–76, 79–80
Internet searches in, xiv, 29, 43–45, 52, 54
preparation for, 2–3, 41
proactive, for what you really want, 57–65
traits needed for, xi–xii, xii, 2–3, 7, 8–10, 8*f,* 41 (*see also* Predator traits)

Job offers, 73, 81
counter offer on compensation *vs.,* 111–112, 119
negotiation and, 110, 149, 178
personality adjustments and, 97, 176
what to expect in, 107–118, 121–130

Job opportunities, 44–49, 57, 70
finding, through online "boards," 44–45, 53
using LinkedIn for, 45–49

Job placement programs, 18, 20
publicly funded, 14, 23

Job Seeker service, 48

Job skills, xiii–xiv, 13
assessment of, xiv, 21, 22, 54–55, 58, 59*f,* 116–117 (*see also* Skill development)
executive, 28–29 (*see also* Strategic skills development process)
general, in mature candidates, 21–26, 29
hard *vs.* soft types of, 31–33
little-to-no, xiv, 13–20, 29
marketable, and advantage, 21, 45, 174
specific, lacking in college grads, 20–21, 29
specific and advanced labor, 27–28, 29, 43–65

Job titles, 84
ascertain, 75, 108–109, 118
change in, as strategic career moves, 141–142
fair market value exists for all, 87–88
industry and, 21, 45

Job training
community colleges and, 15, 19*f*
employers and, 20, 22
re-training as, for mature candidates, 23, 24, 29

MBA (Master of Business Administration) degrees, 82
  as qualification for management, 135*f*, 136
  resumé building with, 21, 140, 141*f*
McKinsey & Company (firm), 82
Mediation, 148
Meditation, benefits of, 168, 170
Memorandum of understanding (MOU), 148, 149, 154
Meta tags, 52
Microquest Directory, 63
Mindset, 114
  preparation as, 3, 11, 68, 97, 99
  second interview and, 97, 99
Minimum wage jobs, little-to-no job skills and, xiv, 13, 14–15
Misconduct, 128
Mistaken identity, 102
Money, 17
  power *vs.,* as objective, 126–127, 130, 142, 176
  See also Compensation levels
Monster.com, 44, 53
MOU (Memorandum of understanding), 148, 149, 154
MSN.com, 70

N

Negotiation strategy and tactics, 147–153, 177
  process of, 152–153, 155
  strategy types for offers, 153, 155
  structure and philosophy of, 149–151, 154
  tactics, 78, 110
  take-aways from experience in, 36, 147–148
  tools in scope of, 148–149, 154
Networking, 27, 137
  professional and social online, sites, 43, 44–45, 104–105, 117, 175
  social, and resumé building, 140, 141*f*
Neuro Linguistic Programming, 11
Nicholson, Jack, actor, 10

O

Oliver, Vicky, author, 85
On-the-job training, 20
"One Flew Over The Cuckoo's Nest" (film), take-aways from, 10
101 great answers to the toughest interview questions (Fry), 85

W

Websites, 70
 building personal, and
   branding, 50–52,
   51*f,* 55
 salary, as candidate
   resource, 109, 111
 SEO principles in building
   your own, 52–53,
   54
Wordtacker.com, 52
Work ethic, 39
 references to verify, and
   traits, 33*f,* 38, 40
 as subjective soft skill, 32,
   33, 33*f,* 76, 174
Workflow
 cross-training in, and
   resumé building,
   140, 141*f*
 diagram, of target
   companies, 69, 77,
   79*f*
 interactive discussion of, as
   negotiating tactic,
   78, 98, 104, 175,
   178
Workforce, skill categories in,
   136, 174
Workshops, 144

Y

Yahoo Finance
 company financial data on,
   60, 70
 as online resource for
   company research,
   44, 53, 58, 62

YouTube.com, 52, 102

Z

ZoomInfo.com, as online
   resource for company
   research, 44, 53.58,
   60, 62

Made in the USA
Charleston, SC
31 March 2013